CROSSING THE CARING BRIDGE – A JOURNEY OF HOPE AND DESPAIR

AUTHORED BY: SHELLY FLAMMIA GREER
EDITED BY: CATHLEEN CANNEY
COVER DESIGN BY: RENEE DAVIS
PREPARED FOR PUBLICATION BY: BARBARA SHAW

ISBN: 1502859416
ISBN-13: 9781502859419
Library of Congress Control Number: 2014919032
CreateSpace Independent Publishing Platform
North Charleston, South Carolina

I dedicate this book to Aynsley and Mary Chandler,
the loves of my life.

1

PROLOGUE

I AM A BLESSED woman. I am not special. I am no different from the next person. I am a daughter, sister, cousin, wife, daughter-in-law, sister-in-law, aunt, mother, mother-in-law, grandmother, and friend. I am a person of deep faith, and never has my faith been tested more than during the 18 months from September 1, 2010 to March 9, 2012.

After witnessing a month of uncharacteristic and what I would describe as bizarre behavior, the unimaginable happened: my 61-yr-old husband Phil was diagnosed with a malignant brain tumor. What follows is our story...a chronological history of Phil's struggle with the most aggressive of all brain tumors: a glioblastoma multiforme (GBM).

This book is not meant to be one that describes a "typical" experience, because every situation is different. Every tumor experience has its own unique qualities and challenges. However, this book does chronicle our experience, in the hopes that others living with this diagnosis, or one that is similar, might find comfort in what we learned along the way.

Once we received Phil's diagnosis, all I wanted was someone to tell me what we could expect. What I learned was that no one was equipped to tell me the path that Phil's illness would take, not because we didn't have the best medical staff one could hope for, but because all tumors are different, as is each person's journey through this illness. I was to find out that there were symptoms characteristic of GBMs, but the main determinant was the location of the tumor and the direction in which it grew. The brain is truly a "master organ." As agonizing as it was to watch Phil from the first symptom until the last, it was astounding to witness how one organ controlled his entire life...how he felt, acted, moved, and responded to others. One of the hardest aspects of Phil's entire journey for me personally was the challenge to separate the man from the disease. As much as I would like to say that I got my old Phil back after his initial surgery, he was never the same again. Although his personality changes were not evident to most people, having known Phil since I was 16 years old and having been married to him since I was 20 years old, it was obvious to me that he was no longer the man I had married and never would be again. I tried so hard to believe that he was, but the solicitous, chivalrous, loving and caring man I knew and loved was but a memory after his initial symptoms. A GBM had stolen everything: my husband, our dreams, and our future. A wife lost her husband, children lost their father, grandchildren lost their grandfather, a mother lost her son, sisters lost their brother, and friends lost a friend. Phil's journey was a slow, arduous process, but the one thing that stood out was his indomitable spirit. Never once did he ask why me, why us? He simply maintained. We all did.

2

A Match Made
at a Gas Station

DURING THE MID-TO-LATE 60s when I attended Needham Broughton High School in Raleigh, North Carolina, students both male and female joined "social clubs." They were modeled after the Greek system in colleges and universities in that the different clubs held teas, parties, etc to get to know prospective members. It was like attending "pseudo rush" parties. After going through the process, I joined "The Belvederes." As much as I would like to say that we participated in fund-raising activities to serve our community, we did not. Instead, we raised money to subsidize our trips to the beach: Senior Weekend and for the week following the end of the school year. On a Saturday in January of 1967, I was fulfilling my Belvedere fund-raising responsibilities by selling boxes of Krispy Kreme doughnuts. I didn't want to spend my entire day selling doughnuts, so I tried to think of places where I could go and sell multiple boxes at one time. I decided gas stations would be a good place to start, so I fired up my white, push-button Valiant and made my way to my first stop: Five Points Gulf! When I drove up to the station, out walked a familiar face, one which I associated with being arrogant and stuck on himself. This guy had been quite the athlete before an injury ended his football and basketball careers. Fearing the rejection I was sure I was going to receive, I wanted to melt into the background. I was pleasantly surprised when Phil Greer bought a dozen doughnuts from me. My preconceived ideas about him were totally wrong. He was incredibly polite and soft spoken, not to mention drop-dead handsome! He didn't hesitate to pull out his wallet to help my cause. I was to find out later that Five Points Gulf was his place of employment where he earned $10 each Saturday to fund his social life for the week! A week after I sold Phil that dozen doughnuts, he called and asked me out. That was the beginning of our 45-year love story.

Phil was 2 years older than I but just one grade ahead of me. He graduated in the spring of 1967 and enrolled in the University of North Carolina at Chapel Hill. If I didn't have cheerleading practice, a game to attend, or some other after-school activity, my good friend Jane and I would drive to Chapel Hill to see our respective boyfriends, even if it was just for an hour. We always made it back to Raleigh in time for supper, so our parents never knew of our after-school trips. We made it through Phil's freshman year in college and my senior year in high school, our relationship strong, in spite of the distance involved. We wrote letters to each other every night since a phone call between Raleigh and Chapel Hill was considered "long distance," and cost money!

In the fall of 1968, I entered Peace College, a small girls' school in Raleigh, as a day student. My mother had died 3 years earlier, and since my services were needed at home, I agreed to live off- campus my freshman year. Being a day student was hard, as there was no way to form the close relationships that come from living in a dorm and having a roommate. I felt as though I were still in high school, yet all of my friends were somewhere else. My ultimate goal was to get to UNC-Chapel Hill. After I completed my first semester at Peace, I talked to my father about transferring to another school for my sophomore year. He agreed, so I applied to the University of North Carolina in Greensboro and was accepted. My high school friend, Jane, was there, so we made plans to room together. In September of 1969, we began our first and only semester together at UNC-G! In the late fall, we began hearing rumors that UNC-Chapel Hill needed female students to fill a quota in order to receive government subsidies. Without consulting my father, I phoned the admissions office at UNC-CH, told them my grades, and was accepted over the phone! After I received my acceptance, Jane did the exact same thing! In a matter of 10 minutes, we were planning our move to Chapel Hill and our awaiting boyfriends!! We weren't sure how we were going to break the news to our parents, but our individual goals had been met: both of us would be starting the second semester of our sophomore year as UNC Tarheels!

Phil and I had talked at length about getting married, and we decided to tell our parents over Christmas break in December of 1969. Combining my news about my acceptance to UNC along with my plans to marry Phil was going to require a lot of explaining on my part. We had looked at the calendar and decided that August 2, 1970 would be our wedding date. However, Uncle Sam had other plans. On December 1, 1969, the Selective Service System of the United States conducted the first draft lottery to determine the order of call to military service in the Vietnam War for men born from 1944 to 1950. Jane and I were glued to the television in our dorm room at UNC-G as the lottery began. The third birth date called was December 30, 1948, Phil Greer's birthday!! I couldn't believe my eyes! I immediately picked up the phone and called Phil. He was at his fraternity house oblivious to what had just transpired. The only good thing coming from that night was Phil's winnings from the draft pool at the Sigma Nu House!! He had the lowest number among his fraternity brothers, which meant upon graduation from college, he was sure to be drafted. He and many of his friends donned army attire and marched down Franklin Street in Chapel Hill while I sat in my dorm room trying to figure out what this all meant.

I found out the next day what Phil had decided to do when he informed me of his plans to go to Raleigh and sign up for the Army Reserves. By joining the reserves, he was guaranteed that he would not have to go to Vietnam. He would have to go through basic training and advanced infantry training, which would take a little over 4 months to complete, but he would not serve outside the United States. Selfishly, all I was concerned about was my wedding date. When Phil learned that he would have to go for his training the next summer, we changed our wedding date from August 2, 1970 to December 19, 1970.

Phil missed the first semester of his senior year at UNC while he completed his Army Reserve training. He came home on December 5, 1970, and we were married exactly two weeks later on December 19, 1970. We continued our lives together for the next 41 years.

3

SUMMER 2010

IN THE SPRING of 2010, knowing the opportunity may never present itself again, I chose to accept an early retirement package from GlaxoSmithKline, the company for which I had worked for more than 19 years. By accepting the package, not only would I be entitled to severance pay, but also insurance coverage at no cost for my husband Phil and me for the next 10 months. It was simply too good a deal to pass up. June 11, 2010 was my last day of work, and Phil and I celebrated that night by having supper at Casa Carbone, our favorite Italian restaurant. After we had finished our meal, I asked him to take me to the Apple store where I proceeded to buy myself a retirement present, a new MacBook Pro. Along with the laptop computer, I also purchased a plan that would enable me to take as many computer classes as I would like for the next 12 months. I had never worked on a Macintosh before, only a PC, so I was excited to begin the learning process. Life couldn't have been better. I dreamed of redefining myself in my new role as a "retiree." That night when we went to bed, I remember turning to Phil and saying, "If we're really, really lucky, we may have 20 more years on this earth. Let's make the most of it!" Little did I know that life as I knew it was about to radically change.

I wasted no time in trying to learn all I could about my new Mac computer. I signed up for classes at the Apple Store, and my education began. Sometimes I scheduled two classes a week. I felt like a sponge soaking up all the information I could as I sat one on one with different instructors who shared their vast computer knowledge with me. I loved every minute of my new-found computer knowledge! In addition to having time to take classes, I suddenly found myself available to participate in activities that I previously would have had to decline due to work responsibilities. One invitation I accepted would prove to be an unexpected gift.

I have played in the same bridge club for more than 30 years, and I consider the members my closest friends. A few of the girls in the club have second homes at the beach, and every summer, plans are made to spend a few days together at one of their beach houses. I was so excited to finally be able to go on one of these getaways, since I no longer had to worry about my work schedule. My best friend Courtney Ryon also made the trip. We were staying at a house in Emerald Isle, North Carolina owned by our friends Jeanne and Tom Andrus and Sherry and Rick Wathern. Their house is a few blocks from the ocean, so one of them usually drives the others to the beach along with all of the chairs, umbrellas and other beach necessities. After unloading, they go back to the cottage, exchange the car for a bicycle, and ride back to the beach. When it's time to call it a day, the entire process is repeated in reverse.

On our first day in Emerald Isle, Sherry offered to drive Courtney and me to the beach. On our way, I happened to ask how the real estate market was on the island. With that, Sherry volunteered to drive us by a house that was advertised as being the "cheapest on the island." I viewed the exterior of the house from the car, thanked her for showing it to us, and we drove on to the public beach access where we were dropped off.

It was a beautiful day to be on the beach! The usual conversation that centered around family updates, the latest best sellers, plans for the summer as well as idle chatter, was interrupted by questions about the house that Sherry had shown to us. Courtney had written down the contact information on the "for sale" sign and after much coaxing from her, Sherry decided to call and arrange a time for us to view the property.

It didn't take long for the entire bridge club to take a tour of the beach house and offer up all kinds of opinions from suggested wall colors to potential structural changes to make it a very special place for someone. In no time, Courtney was suggesting to me that we call our husbands and tell them about the deal we had discovered. Phil and I had known Courtney's husband Dan since our days at the University of North Carolina in Chapel Hill. In fact, Phil and Dan were Sigma Nu Fraternity brothers, and since I spent much time at the fraternity house, I counted Dan as one of my dear friends, as well. I quickly reminded Courtney that Phil had no interest in buying a beach house and that his response would not just be "no," but "hell no!"

Our conversation was on Thursday. I returned back home to Raleigh on Friday afternoon as Dan was on his way down to Emerald Isle. Courtney and Dan were spending the weekend with some friends who just happened to be realtors. It wasn't long before Courtney reported back to me that their realtor friends had gone with them to look at the beach house. They gave their opinions that the house was a great buy; the following Monday, Phil agreed to go in with Dan and Courtney to purchase a beach house sight unseen. Even now, I find it hard to believe that Phil went along with the plan without so much as questioning the impulsiveness of the decision. The loan was approved, and we were scheduled to close on the beach house on Friday, August 27, 2010.

Our older daughter Aynsley Armstrong, her husband Cade, and their children live in Montgomery, Alabama. After Aynsley and Cade started having children, we decided to vacation as a family on the panhandle of Florida. Although it's a 12-hour drive from Raleigh, it's only a 3-hour drive for the Armstrongs, which makes traveling with small children a lot easier.

The summer of 2010 was no different from the previous seven summers; we would be vacationing the first week in August in Seagrove, Florida, a quiet family beach about 20 miles east of Destin, Florida.

Aynsley and Cade had a wedding to attend the weekend we were to begin our vacation, so the plan was for Phil and me to travel to Montgomery on Friday, pick up our 3 grandchildren, and head to Florida on Saturday. Aynsley and Cade would join us on Sunday. At the time, Mary Weldon was 7, Greer was 6, and Martha was 2. As planned, Phil and I arrived in Montgomery Friday night, relieved the babysitter, and took over the responsibility of caring for our grandchildren.

The next morning, our trip to the beach with the grandchildren began. It was during this trip that I first began to notice that Phil was exhibiting some strange behavior.

As we headed down the Troy Highway towards our destination, everyone was so excited to be together! Shortly after we left, I asked Phil to stop at a convenience store so that I could get a soft drink. Normally, he would stop at the first available location; however, he seemed to ignore my request. After passing convenience store after convenience store without him stopping, I became aggravated and insisted that he pull into the next available gas station or convenience store for me. His behavior was so out of character for Phil as he always respected any request I made to stop. I finally got my Coke, and we continued on.

As we made our way towards Florida, Phil began obsessing over listening to music through a set of earphones connected to his iPad, the new electronic toy he had purchased right before we had left on vacation. He was constantly repositioning his iPad, which concerned me because of the effect it was having on his driving. I found myself constantly asking him to unplug his iPad and just listen to the radio. He said he was bothered by all the noise in the car! Phil adored our grandchildren, but his patience was growing thin after being with them for just a very short time. It was all I could do to tolerate his behavior as we drove down the road. I was relieved to check into our cottage and put some distance between Phil and the grandchildren and ME.

The vacation was a lot of fun. During our stay, both of our daughters announced that they were expecting babies! The new additions were due a week apart in February 2011. We were all so excited and talked with great anticipation of the two cousins being born so close together! However, in the midst of all the fun we were having, we began to notice that Phil was exhibiting some behavior that seemed out-of-character for him.

One night as we gathered at a local restaurant for supper, Phil again became obsessed with his iPad. Not only was it bizarre that he had brought his iPad with him, but he also seemed to be fixated on it as we all tried to eat. He was totally disengaged from conversation at the table, which was unlike him. After expressing my frustration with his obsessive-compulsive behavior, he got up from the table and went to the bar of the restaurant. When he returned, I asked him what he was doing at the bar to which he responded "trying to find an Internet connection." When I asked him why he felt the need to be connected to the Internet, he said he wanted to read WRAL news to see what was happening in Raleigh. I assured him that if there were something of major importance going on in Raleigh, my brother or sister would let us know. However, that did not slow his quest of finding a WiFi connection. It was not like Phil to obsess about technology, and certainly not when we were spending time together as a family. I could not understand what was driving this behavior and was relieved to leave the restaurant and return to the cottage.

Unfortunately, Phil's obsession with electronics did not end there.

Sometime during the week, he learned that Verizon was coming out with a new smart phone called the "Droid." He made it his mission to find out where he could purchase one of these phones, calling as far away as Texas.

When our week in Seagrove came to an end, we packed up into the three cars we had driven and headed back to Montgomery. My younger daughter, Mary Chandler, and her husband Scott rode with Phil. Their trip back took an unexpected turn when Phil made the decision to stop at a local Verizon store to see about purchasing the "Droid." He insisted that they stop, and they spent two hours in the Verizon store before leaving empty handed. I was both incredulous and irritated when I heard what Phil had done! However, we quickly moved on with our last night together before having to return home. Mary Chandler, Scott, Phil and I headed back to North Carolina the next day, and the rest of the trip was uneventful. However, in the days and weeks to come, Phil began acting more and more unlike himself, and I began to worry.

4

WHO IS THIS PERSON?

ONCE HOME FROM our vacation, I began busying myself with ideas for the beach house. Courtney and I talked frequently about plans for decorating and furnishing our new vacation getaway. Courtney, who is well-versed in consignment shopping, led the way in our search for affordable decor. We were successful in finding some of the furniture and accessories, but we still needed to furnish our living room and dining room. In order to do it expeditiously, Courtney and I decided to take a "day trip" to the coast to complete our shopping. We spoke with friends who also had second homes in Emerald Isle and took their advice as to where to begin our search.

By 3:00, our frustration level had reached its peak. Not only had we not seen anything we liked, the furniture we did see was so beyond our budget that we were beginning to think our trip was in vain. At this point, we decided to head 20 miles east to Morehead City to try one last store. When we walked into the family-owned furniture store, we were greeted by an attractive young woman who looked at us and said "You ladies look like you need help."

Our faces must have had frustration and exhaustion written all over them! We confirmed her observation, gave her our budget and asked if there was anything in her store that would come close to fulfilling our needs. Unbeknownst to us, we had been met by the owner of the store.

In 90 minutes, she helped us with our selections, ensured that we were staying within our budget, and arranged for delivery on the day we were closing on the house. As we left the store, Courtney and I high-fived each other, got in the car, and headed back to Raleigh. As we pulled out of the parking lot, I received a phone call from Phil.

He was worried that we were going to be driving in severe weather. There were tornado watches and warnings in the northeast part of the state but nowhere near where we were driving. I thanked him for his concern and assured him we were fine. When I finished talking to him, I commented to Courtney how weird it was that he was worried about the weather; however, I dismissed it at the time, and we drove back home to Raleigh.

However, during the two weeks between my shopping trip with Courtney and the closing date for our beach house on August 27, 2010, Phil continued to exhibit strange behavior. For example, one morning he got up, went into the bathroom and started the shower. He then inexplicably went to another bathroom in the house. When I asked him about it, he said he was "letting the water warm up," which of course made no sense. I was beginning to lose patience with his strange behavior, never thinking there could be an organic reason for it. In retrospect, I wonder how I was able to rationalize Phil's actions with his reasoning at the time. Perhaps it was a form of denial; I just don't know. But I think about it a lot now.

During the month of August, Phil also developed another symptom. He began getting up three and four times a night to go to the bathroom. My first thought was that he might be having an issue with his prostate, so at my urging, he made an appointment with his urologist for Tuesday, August 31, 2010.

On August 27, our closing date for the beach house finally arrived. In order to move all the furnishings from Raleigh to the beach, it was necessary to rent a truck. The plan was for Dan and Phil to leave at 6:30 am, with Phil driving the truck and Dan following behind in his car. Phil Greer had always been the most punctual person I knew, so when he did not make the 6:30 time, it gave me pause and also aggravated me a bit. It seemed that Phil was just piddling around making Dan wait, which was so unlike Phil that it added to my list of concerns about his behavior. They finally left a little after 7:00, and Courtney and I left shortly thereafter.

The closing went off without a hitch. Phil had arranged everything, and he was in total control of the process, not surprising since mortgage loans were his expertise. Observing his performance in the attorney's office was reassurance for me that he was doing OK...that he must just be distracted by the preparation and execution of the closing on a vacation home. Phil was totally on top of his game that day. Unfortunately, any reassurances I had been given from closing day would be short-lived.

After the closing, we grabbed a quick lunch and headed to the beach house to meet the crew that Phil had arranged to come help unload all of the contents of the truck. Phil was totally disengaged from this part of the process. He just walked around watching all of the activity. In fact, at one point, he sat down and took a nap. Removing himself from the activity was completely out-of-character from the Phil I knew. I would normally have to remind him that we were paying people to do the work that he insisted on helping with. The Phil I knew would have been right in the middle of it all. Instead, it was as if he were in another world.

One of the most worrisome things that happened that day centered around the television. We were unable to get the TV to work, and Phil was not the least bit interested in helping to determine what was wrong. His lack of concern and perceived inability to diagnose the problem did not add up because Phil, at one time, was in the TV and appliance business, and he knew a lot about TVs and how to set them up. I can still see him sitting in the middle of the living room floor holding the remote and doing nothing. I pleaded with him to work his magic, and he just sat there and said he did not know what was wrong. After a while, Phil finally took Dan and drove him all over Onslow county looking for a new TV. They finally returned with a new flat screen TV, and after a call to the cable company, we were in business.

We had a great weekend, and I tried to ignore the quirky things Phil was doing. At the time, I think I was trying my best to justify the subtle personality changes I was observing, because as time went by, I was becoming more and more concerned.

That Sunday was the day that confirmed for me that something was wrong. The plan was for Phil and Dan to return to Raleigh, Phil driving the truck and Dan following him. Courtney and I were going to stay until Tuesday, so that we could stock the pantry and purchase items we had not thought about needing before we moved in the beach house. Right after lunch, Phil went to the truck, got in, backed out of the driveway, and started driving down the road. He did this without telling anyone his plans. I ran after him screaming for him to stop! When I got to the truck, I asked him why he was leaving as Dan was not ready to go. I also asked why he had left without telling me good-bye, which was not normal behavior for him. He would never have left without kissing me good-bye and making sure that I had some money. Although, in my heart, I knew something was dreadfully wrong, I allowed myself to justify his behavior. He was eager to return home and rest up before the start of the work week. He left the beach, driving back to Raleigh without Dan following him.

Five hours after Phil left Emerald Isle I had not heard a word from him. The drive from the beach house to our home in Raleigh is two and one-half hours. I called his cell phone every five minutes, but he didn't answer. Another friend from Raleigh who was in Emerald Isle for the weekend was heading back home late Sunday afternoon. I called her, explained what was going on, and asked that she keep her eye out for Phil. At this point, I was afraid he had been in an accident. Six hours after Phil left Emerald Isle, I finally heard from him. It seems he had stopped at a Verizon store in Jacksonville, NC to have his phone checked, and when he left, he got turned around and ended up taking a longer route home. Again, I somehow was able to accept his explanation because he made it believable. He said when he realized he was going the wrong way, he chose a route that would take him through Kinston, NC so he could pick up a Bar-B-Q sandwich at one of our favorite Bar-B-Q restaurants. He apologized for any worry he had caused, and we ended our conversation. Dan had told me earlier in the day that he thought Phil was just tired and stressed over all of the recent activity and not to worry. As hard as it was for me to believe that Phil was stressed, I did so as a means of calming my fears. However, my acceptance of Dan's explanation would soon be shattered.

During the next few days, Courtney and I worked feverishly to get everything done that we hoped to accomplish before we had to leave the beach. We enjoyed ourselves as we shopped, cleaned and turned our beach house into a beach home. We shared dreams we had for our new little cottage. For a little while, it was easy not to think about Phil and the implications of his strange behavior.

On Tuesday morning, we got up, packed the car, and began our trip home to Raleigh. It was August 31, 2010, the day Phil was scheduled to see his urologist. His appointment was scheduled for 9:45 that morning. As I drove home, I decided to call Phil and make sure he remembered his appointment. At this point, it was 9:00. I called his office phone first, and his secretary told me he had not come into the office yet. I tried his cell phone but got no answer. My last attempt was our home phone and again, there was no answer. At this point, I was becoming concerned, but I was trying to keep my emotions in check.

I called my next-door neighbor Robin Pauli and asked if she would look out her door to see if Phil's car was in the driveway. She confirmed that it was and she said "Shelly, the newspaper is still at the end of your driveway." My heart sank. I was afraid that something terrible had happened to Phil. In a matter of seconds, my mind raced with thoughts of a heart attack, stroke, cerebral hemorrhage. I KNEW something was wrong. Robin agreed to go over to our house to see if Phil would answer the doorbell. It wasn't long before she called me back to say that Phil had in fact answered the door and was alive and well. Shortly after that, Phil called. I expressed my concern and his response was contrite. I reminded him of his 9:45 appointment. He told me his plan was to go to the office and address some work issues and then go to his appointment. I tried to be gentle as I told him he did not have time for all of that since his office was 20 minutes away. He disagreed, and the conversation ended.

I felt sick. As I continued to drive down the road, I asked Courtney to take out paper and pen, and together, we proceeded to make a list of all of the bizarre things Phil had said and done over the past 6 weeks. I was convinced it was time to call the doctor; I would do so as soon as I arrived home.

5

THE DIAGNOSIS

"...It's not good news. You have a primary malignant brain tumor in the right frontal lobe of your brain. You're going to need a neurosurgeon...."

At 10:45 AM on September 1, 2010, I picked Phil up from his office, and we drove to his internist's office for an 11:00 am appointment. I felt so bad for Phil as he listened to me describe his strange behavior to the nurse. He was not aware that he was acting any differently than he normally acted. When the nurse began asking him questions regarding the date, the president, the season, the next holiday, etc., he answered every question correctly except for the date. I sat there hoping against hope that everything would be OK. The doctor came in the room, talked to us, examined Phil, and then sent him across the hall for a CT Scan.

It was no time before the doctor called us back into his office to say that something had shown up on the Scan and that he had arranged for Phil to have an MRI. The CT Scan could not differentiate between a tumor or a bleed, but the MRI could. When Phil was called back by the MRI technician, I was left alone to sit and think about what had transpired during the previous two hours. An ominous feeling came over me, and I decided to make two phone calls.

The first call went to Courtney. As luck would have it, she held the position of Manager of the Special Constituent Program at Duke University Medical Center and was well versed in the newly diagnosed brain tumor protocols. I quickly brought her up to date, and she advised me to get Phil's MRI put on a disk. In the event that we would need a neurosurgeon, she scheduled an appointment with Dr. Alan Friedman, a world-renowned physician at Duke. We could always cancel if necessary.

The second call I made was to Jim Blaine, president of the N.C. State Employees' Credit Union, and a personal friend. Again, I found myself trying to explain what was going on and the fear that was beginning to overcome me. I promised to update him as I learned more about Phil's situation. During this time, I was also texting our two daughters, Aynsley who lives in Montgomery, AL and Mary Chandler who lives in Greensboro, NC, trying to give them a play-by-play report. Once Phil's scan was completed, we got in the car and began driving home to await a call from the doctor. We were halfway home when Phil received a call from his doctor asking that we come back to his office. I knew then we were not going to hear the news we wanted to hear. What an understatement.

When we arrived back at the doctor's office, we were quickly ushered into an exam room. There was no sugar coating anything. The doctor walked into the room and said "It's not good news. You have a primary malignant brain tumor in the right frontal lobe of your brain. You're going to need a neurosurgeon."

Phil and I both sat there speechless. The doctor looked right at Phil and told him he would probably have the tumor removed, have a little radiation and then be good to go. I explained to the doctor that Phil already had an appointment scheduled to see Dr. Friedman September 3, 2010, so it would not be necessary for his staff to call a neurosurgeon. The doctor then told us that he was sorry, and we left the office. We got back in the car, and I began driving home.

"Well, shit!" That's all I could say. Waves of nausea came over me. We drove home in silence, both of us paralyzed by the news we had just heard. Thoughts, emotions, and fears were flying in and out of my brain so fast I couldn't process them! What did this all mean? The rational, intellectual side was clear...my husband had just been given a devastating diagnosis. Selfishly, I was thinking, "What would this mean for me? How am I going to handle this? Phil was my anchor. I couldn't imagine life without him. Who would take care of me and our children and grandchildren? How were we going to tell his elderly mother the news? Would his illness affect our financial stability? Was Phil going to be dead in a matter of weeks, months, years? It was all about me, me, me!"

As I continued driving, I looked over at Phil. He was staring straight ahead, his face emotionless. My selfish thinking suddenly turned into absolute horror and empathy. What must Phil be thinking after hearing such sickening and terrifying news? Phil and his family were known for their stoicism. His reaction to his diagnosis, although hard to understand, was exactly as one would have expected.

Once we arrived home, I knew the next step would be telling family and friends, and I dreaded the thought. If we repeated the news we had just been given, it must be true. I wanted to drop Phil off, back the car out of the driveway, and drive until I could not drive anymore. The reality of the situation was taking hold.

6

THE WAIT

WORD SPREAD QUICKLY, and before we knew it, friends and family descended upon us to offer love and support. Mary Chandler and Scott came from Greensboro and brought supper. Conversation was light. Until our appointment with Dr. Friedman on Friday, we would not know what it was we were dealing with other than a cursory diagnosis of a malignant brain tumor.

For the next day and a half, Phil and I both busied ourselves with routine tasks. Phil went to work at the N.C. State Employees' Credit Union where he had worked for the past 30 years and faced the daunting task of informing his employees about his medical condition. I felt so sorry for him. I knew it was not going to be easy for him to have to tell his entire staff about what the doctors had found. He would not have any details to share until after his appointment at Duke, and I knew his friends and colleagues would be crestfallen.

I cleaned the house, shopped for groceries, and ran the necessary errands required to keep a household going. I began identifying which people I needed to inform about Phil's illness and what activities I needed to postpone or cancel. I began with the gym, where I placed my membership on hold until I had further knowledge of our situation. While there, I ran into my kick-boxing instructor, Kris. Until I saw her, I had not cried. I could not get the words out about Phil before I fell into her arms and sobbed. I hardly knew Kris, but somehow falling apart in the presence of someone other than a family member or close friend felt safe to me.

When I arrived at my next destination, the nail salon, I experienced the same level of decompensation. Again, confiding in someone I did not know well about my husband's life-threatening disease resulted in my crying uncontrollably. Diem had just opened her own nail salon, and I was so excited to be supporting her efforts; however, I knew that having my nails done on a regular basis was no longer a priority. In Vietnamese, she informed the others working in the salon of my news. The love and compassion of the women in that salon transcended the language barrier, and they each consoled me.

Time seemed to stand still that week. Friday could not get here fast enough. I wanted so badly to talk to Phil about what he was thinking...his fears, his worries, but he never said a thing. Phil was never one to express concern over anything, and this time was no different. I wanted him to tell me how afraid he was of a very precarious future at best. I wanted to comfort him, which in turn would have lead to his comforting me. He would have given me a pat on the leg to assure me that everything was going to be fine. For some reason, even though I knew better, I would have believed him. That ever-so-assuring pat was all I needed, but it never came.

As we all continued to dance around the reality of Phil's condition, Friday, September 3, 2010 finally arrived. My brother Dayle had offered to take us to Duke and be present as we spoke with Dr. Friedman. Dayle is an attorney and is well versed in taking detailed

notes in depositions, so I welcomed his offer. Knowing that someone else was responsible for the details, freed me to listen and ask
questions.

Dr. Friedman entered his office, introduced himself, and
shook our hands as we introduced ourselves. He immediately
walked to his desk, sat down, and placed the CD of Phil's MRI
into his computer. I watched as he pulled up each slice of the
MRI that showed a round, white mass in Phil's brain. He would
enlarge the view and then take it back to its original size. He sat
there looking and not saying a word. Phil, Dayle, and I just sat
there waiting for his response. He finally turned around and said
"Well, you have a tumor and it's got to come out." I asked if it was
a glioblastoma, and he told me he thought so, but that he would
not know for sure until he removed it. With that, he pulled out
a personal calendar from the pocket of his lab coat and began
looking at dates. The first date he offered was 2 weeks away. He
looked at Phil and seemed to read the disappointment on his
face. He looked down at his calendar again and said "Monday is
Labor Day, and I have that day off. I can do it then. I operated
on one of the Osmond Brothers on Labor Day; no reason I can't
do the same for you." We jumped at his offer and thanked him
profusely.

We were then referred to his PA, Jay, who schooled us on what
to expect, where to be and when. We completed the necessary
paperwork and then made our way to radiology for a CT scan and
another MRI to rule out cancer in any other locations in Phil's
body. After the additional testing, Phil, Dayle, and I drove back to
Raleigh, exhausted from a day that had been spent asking questions and seeking answers.

There is something reassuring about having a plan of action,
and we were anxious to put the plan in motion. Monday could not
get here soon enough.

Aynsley, Mary Chandler, and I knew there would be many people wanting details and updates on Phil's condition. We needed to come up with a means of communication that would not involve countless phone calls and/or e-mails. We also were keenly aware of how details can get lost in translation, so we wanted to ensure that accurate information was being delivered.

It was Aynsley's idea to create a Caring Bridge site that we could keep updated to let friends and loved ones know exactly what was going on. Since she is more computer savvy than I, she set up the site, and we agreed to keep it current, thereby eliminating rumors that invariably get started by hearsay. In retrospect, there could not have been a better idea. Not only did the site keep people up-to-date on Phil's condition, but it also served as a diary of Phil's journey.

Knowing that Phil would be reading my posts on the Caring Bridge site, I made the decision to keep it as positive and upbeat as possible. It would be a place of factual information as well as one of faith and hope. What it would not reveal would be my true feelings, my doubts, and my fears. Little did I know how much it would mean to Phil. As I updated the site, people would make comments and send good wishes to Phil. He treasured every comment and read them over and over again.

In the beginning of the chapters that follow, I will provide all of the actual posts from the Caring Bridge site, just as they appeared. I'll also be disclosing my thoughts and feelings, something I had to be careful to keep to myself. I was committed to being Phil's beacon of hope. I was always full of positive feedback that I was counting on to be the catalyst to keep him fighting.

Because of the love that Phil and I shared for all sports, especially football, I decided to approach my entries as if we were on a football team, readying ourselves for the upcoming season that would include many a foe on the other side of the ball. My writing became cathartic, and I found that what I was writing was not far from the truth. We were on a team where everyone involved was intent on winning!

7

THE SURGERY

September 4, 2010, 5:59pm

On Friday, September 3rd, Phil was seen by Dr. Alan Friedman at Duke. Dr. Friedman will operate on Monday, September 6th at 7:30 am to remove the tumor. At that time, we will know more information about the type and grade. Hopefully, he will be back home by Thursday.

OK, so now we had a date and time for Phil's surgery; we just needed to occupy our minds until it was time to go to Duke. On Saturday morning, September 4, 2010, Phil went through his usual routine of eating breakfast, reading the paper, showering and dressing. Afterwards, he announced that he wanted to go see his mother, his only surviving parent, and tell her what was going on. Phil's father died in 1988, and his mother, Aurelia Greer, lived in the health center of Springmoor Lifecare Retirement Community, in Raleigh. She was 87 years old and had suffered from an undisclosed dementia-type illness for the previous four years. There were days she could carry on a simple conversation, and there were other times when she would just stare at the person speaking to her without saying a word. She always seemed to recognize whoever was there, but you just never knew which Aurelia you would see. I offered to go with Phil to tell her, but he declined; he wanted to do this by himself. I dropped him off at Springmoor and headed to the grocery store with the understanding that he would call when he was ready to come home.

I had just arrived at the store when I received a call from Mary Chandler saying that Phil had already called and was ready to come home. She agreed to pick him up. As Mary Chandler approached Springmoor, she saw Phil on the street walking in the direction of our house. He seemed to be losing his capacity to follow directions, and he was having problems with impulse control. Our house is less than a mile from Springmoor, and it takes about a minute to make the drive. He could not wait long enough for Mary Chandler to make the short trip; he felt compelled to start walking. Again, we were witnessing actions so unlike the Phil we knew. It seemed we were observing further decline in his behavior as each hour passed.

When I returned from the grocery store, I asked him about his visit with his mother. He responded by saying, "Her only words were 'I'm glad you have a good family.'" He did not need to tell me any more. I could tell he was crushed by the response he had received. I don't care how old one is, we all seek the love and comfort only one's mother can provide. Phil's mother no longer had the capacity to offer that comfort.

Later that day, our daughter Aynsley was due to arrive from Montgomery, Alabama. She was driving up to be present for Phil's surgery, and he was looking forward to her arrival. Mary Chandler and Scott had already come to Raleigh from Greensboro. As happy as Phil was to have both his girls with him, I think I was even happier.

Both of our daughters are very bright and level-headed young women. I immediately felt a sense of relief come over me when they walked inside the house. I knew that I would no longer be in this battle alone. I would no longer have to be making decisions on my own. I would have their input and their support. Most of all, I would have their love and emotional support as my role of caregiver was beginning to take hold. I had never felt so immobilized in thought in my life. It's hard to say, but I was reaching a point of not being able to think for myself or anyone else. I wanted so badly to go to sleep and have this nightmare over with! I prayed constantly that I would be shown what it was I was to do next. It was not long before I could not even pray for Phil or anyone else for that matter. I went to bed Saturday night comforted by the fact that Aynsley and Mary Chandler were "home" with us and would be with us as we navigated our way down a very scary path.

September 5, 2010, 7:45pm

Today has been a busy day and brought us one day closer to Phil's surgery. We checked into Duke around 10:30 am after which Dr. Friedman greeted us in the lobby to explain the plan for the next day. He is an incredibly kind individual who shows a keen interest in not only his patient, but also the patient's family. He immediately put us at ease and prepared us for the journey ahead. Once we got to Phil's room, his nurse informed us that it would be late afternoon before any pre-op activities would begin. He advised us to go do something fun that would get us out of the hospital environment for a while. Acting on the nurse's advice, we headed to Chapel Hill for lunch. There's nothing like breathing in clear, crisp air under a Carolina blue sky to soothe one's soul. After a fabulous lunch at "Top of the Hill" (thank you Linda and Cliff!), it was on to Johnny T-shirt to purchase just the right "Carolina" pajamas for Phil to have during his "Duke" experience. When we returned to Duke, Phil began the litany of pre-op tests that had been ordered for him. For supper, Phil requested a meal from Mama Dips, so Mary Chandler, Aynsley, and Scott dutifully headed back to Chapel Hill to fulfill his request. Thanks to Phil, we were all able to enjoy Mama Dip's southern cooking!

As the day draws to an end, we are reminded of our family, our friends, and the many blessings in our lives. Words are not adequate to express our love and gratitude to each of you as you pray for Phil and our family. We know we will be all right regardless of the outcome. We have a deep faith and are confident that God is in charge. We are most grateful that as we jump into this black hole called a brain tumor, you are holding our hands and going with us.

As we always do on Sunday mornings, we attended the early church service at Hayes Barton United Methodist Church in Raleigh, NC. Phil was insistent upon going. I, on the other hand, would have been fine staying at home since it was the morning we were to check into Duke.

The service, scheduled to begin at 8:30, is usually over by 9:30; however, with it being the first Sunday of the month, Communion was being served, which sometimes resulted in the service lasting longer. I knew we had to be at Duke by 10:30, and we would be cutting it close by going to church, but I could not deny Phil's wish to be there.

Aynsley, Mary Chandler, and Scott immediately came up with a plan where they would stay at home and then come to the church to pick us up and take us to Duke. By their coming to the church, it saved us the time it would have taken to go back home to get them. Our minister, Rick Clayton, knew of Phil's plight and had come to our house shortly after receiving word of Phil's diagnosis. We took our usual seats in the sanctuary, third row on the right side. As the rituals of the Sunday morning service proceeded, it came time for announcements. Rick took this time to inform the congregation of what it was that Phil would be facing. It was very emotional, and for the first time in my presence, Phil cried. Taking Communion was another emotional aspect of the service, but what happened next was totally unexpected.

Rick called Phil and me to the front of the church. He invited those people wishing to do so to come forward and join him by placing their hands on us as he prayed. It nearly brought us to our knees.

The love and support we felt from our church family empowered us to leave the comforts of familiar surroundings and head to unfamiliar territory where we were being challenged to learn a new meaning of the word trust.

As Phil checked in at Duke University Medical Center, I was amazed to hear that Dr. Friedman would be coming to the lobby to speak with us! The receptionist told us Dr. Friedman makes an effort to greet all of his patients as they check into the hospital. He likes to get to know the family and let everyone know what to expect the day of surgery.

Although he is a man of few words, Dr. Friedman put everyone at ease and even joked with Aynsley and Mary Chandler. I knew Phil was where he needed to be, and that he was being cared for by one of the most gifted neurosurgeons in the world. Monday could not come fast enough! During our conversation with Dr. Friedman, he explained the risks of surgery. He said Phil should not have personality changes post-op, but that he would probably be "flat" for a while due to the surgery. He also explained that Phil faced the possibility of temporary paralysis on his left side, but it would resolve. We thanked Dr. Friedman and said our good-byes. He said he would see us bright and early the next morning.

Once Phil got to his room and we met the team of nurses, interns, and residents that would be caring for him, we were encouraged to leave the medical center and find something fun to do until late afternoon when his pre-op activities would begin. We decided fun sounded like lunch at "Top of the Hill" on Franklin Street in Chapel Hill. We sat outside and enjoyed both the atmosphere and the food.

When it came time to leave, we started walking toward the elevator. As Phil started to board an elevator alone, I asked that he wait for the rest of our group before going down. I turned my head for just a minute, and the next thing I knew, the elevator door shut, and Phil was headed down by himself. It was as if he was unable to process what I was saying to him. I looked out the window only to see Phil crossing Franklin Street, oblivious to the traffic and to the fact that he was alone.

My heart sank. I felt like I was watching the movie "Regarding Henry" where the brain-damaged character played by Harrison Ford gets lost while walking down the street. Mary Chandler hurried down the stairs, and I continued watching out the window until I saw her reach Phil and guide him safely to the other side of the street. Phil seemed to be getting worse and worse as the day progressed, and I wanted so badly to go back to Duke so that he would be safe in the hospital. Selfishly, I wanted to be relieved of all responsibility of watching Phil's every move. His behavior had continued to deteriorate, and my anxiety level was off the charts. I was scared to death; however, Phil wanted to make one more stop before we headed back to Durham. He wanted to go to Johnny T-Shirt to buy some UNC pajamas to wear during his hospital stay.

In the store, Phil was so confused about what he was buying and whether or not he was entitled to a free T-shirt. It was incredibly difficult for me to watch. Mary Chandler picked up on my anxiety, and she stepped in and handled the situation. Once the shopping had been completed, I insisted that we go back to Duke. I wanted Phil to be among medical professionals, and I wanted someone else to be in charge.

As afternoon turned into evening, Phil was very specific about what he wanted to eat for supper. He requested "southern food" from Mama Dips Kitchen in Chapel Hill. Scott, Mary Chandler, and Aynsley traveled back to Chapel Hill to fulfill Phil's request. Once they returned to the hospital, we took our southern cuisine into the atrium of the hospital and had supper together.

Afterwards, Aynsley, Mary Chandler, and Scott went home to spend the night. Phil and I returned to his room to await the many pre-op activities that were scheduled for him. There were skull x-rays, EKG, EEG, neuro exams, a CT scan, IV steroids for edema prophylaxis, and Keppra for seizure prophylaxis.

September 6, 2010, 1:45pm

Phil's surgery went well, and he is resting comfortably in ICU where he will remain for the next 24 hrs. Dr. Friedman said the tumor appeared to be a glioblastoma, but we will await the final pathology report to confirm his findings. The girls and I visited with him, amazed at how alert he was. His first request was for a sausage biscuit. Thank goodness for Zocor® and Zantac®!! Thank you for continuing to pray.

The night before Phil's surgery was a restless one for me, but thanks to medication, Phil slept soundly that night. I slept off and on.

Most of my time was spent staring at Phil and wondering what was to come. My mind raced. Could the doctors possibly be wrong? Could the tumor be benign? I simply wasn't ready to give up on the hope that it was all going to be OK. Nurses were in and out of the room all night long administering pre-op meds and drawing blood for lab work.

At 5:30, our minister and his wife arrived to offer prayer and support. Aynsley, Mary Chandler and Scott arrived an hour later as we waited for Phil to be taken to the OR. We were invited back to the pre-op area to be with Phil before surgery. While there, we met with Dr. Friedman and the anesthesiologist, who informed us that Phil would be in the pre-op area for about 45 minutes to an hour before they would anesthetize him. They told us that the surgery would take about three hours.

Since it was a holiday, we had the surgical waiting room to ourselves. Family and friends gathered to wait with us, and the conversation helped to pass the time. When the surgery was completed, we were called back to a small conference room to meet with Dr. Friedman. He entered the room and told us there were no surprises, that he had removed the tumor and that Phil had tolerated the procedure very well. I asked him if it was, in fact, a glioblastoma (GBM) and he said yes, but they would still await the pathology report confirming his findings. I asked him what grade the tumor was, and he informed me that all GBMs are stage 4. With that, I said "I wish I had a crystal ball." Dr. Friedman responded "No you don't Shelly...then you would be counting the days. Go out and live your life."

When he left the room, I just sat there, frozen. That's when Aynsley spoke up and made the most profound statement I had heard to date. She said "You know mom, we're all terminal. None of us knows how long we have." Although I knew that Aynsley was correct in her thinking, it confirmed for me that I was not in control of Phil's well-being. All my hopes of the tumor being benign and everything being OK had been dashed. Our lives would never be the same again, but what did that mean? I kept repeating to myself "What am I going to do?"

We left the privacy of our conference room and returned to the waiting room to share the news with the friends and family who had been waiting so patiently. As we left the hospital, Courtney put her arm around me and walked me to the car. I was tearful and repeated to her the same thing I had been saying to myself, "What am I going to do?" She assured me that we would get through this, and that she and Dan would be right there with Phil and me.

We headed home to regroup and prepare to return to Duke to see Phil. At that point, I had been in the same clothes for over 24 hours, so I was looking forward to a shower and the familiar surroundings of my own home.

When we arrived back at Duke, Phil was out of the recovery room and in a bed in neuro-intensive care. I don't know what I was expecting him to look like, but I was surprised when I saw him sitting up in bed, his head wrapped in a bandage that looked like a turban, and talking away. He said he was starving, and that he wanted a sausage biscuit. That request was all it took for Scott to hear. He immediately left the hospital, drove to Bojangles, and got Phil his biscuit!

We took turns visiting Phil, since only two people were allowed to be in the room at a time. Our minister returned later in the afternoon to offer his support. I remember greeting him in the hall outside of the intensive care area. As an aside, I have a very difficult time crying in front of other people and to some, this may seem strange. Rick had not seen me shed a tear. He looked at me and said something to the effect of "Shelly, at some time, you need to come to grips with what you are facing." I responded by assuring him that I did indeed know what I was facing. I also told him that I was a wonderful actress, and that Phil Greer would never see me be anything but positive. I would be his biggest cheerleader! By cheering him on, I would be essentially cheering myself on as well.

I was so overwhelmed by the thought of Phil's prognosis. No healthcare professional had mentioned a word about life expectancy, but I knew what his diagnosis meant. As I sat and watched Phil, I pulled the pashmina that I was wearing around my shoulders tighter and tighter as though I were physically holding myself together. I longed for someone to tell me what to do. As long as Phil was in the hospital, there was still time for me to come up with a plan.

September 7, 2010, 7:41pm

What a difference a day and a good night's sleep makes! Aynsley, Mary Chandler, and I began our day feeling that we were well equipped for whatever we would face today. When we arrived back at the neuro-intensive care unit this morning, we found Phil chomping at the bit to get back on his iPad and to get out of the hospital. When Dr. Friedman made his rounds, he had mentioned to Phil that he was doing so well that he could probably go home today, and Phil took him at his word. When I asked Phil how he had slept, he responded "Great! I walked at 1:00 am, 3:00 am, and 6:00 am." If that's his idea of a good night's sleep, so be it. The rest of the day was spent waiting for him to be transferred out of the intensive care unit to a room on the floor. Finally, at 3:00, Phil got his wish. He WALKED out of the intensive care unit to a regular room. Dr. Friedman came by around 3:30 and confirmed what Phil had reported earlier...after a post-op MRI, he was being sent home! His only order was to shave, because as Dr. Friedman commented, he looked like a bum! Actually, I was beginning to grow fond of his new bearded look. Dr. Friedman also reminded us that as Phil continues on his regimen of steroids for the next couple of weeks, he would be "hyper" and "eat us out of house and home." So with that, I made sure my Costco card was up to date, and I am prepared to buy in bulk! Phil is now resting comfortably at home on his beloved couch with our dogs, Molly and Tapper. With him back home, we can reclaim some semblance of normalcy and prepare ourselves for the fight that lies before us. We will continue to be guided by our team from Duke as to our next steps. Phil will go back in a week to have his staples removed and to meet with the brain tumor team. The girls and I have agreed that none of us, including Phil, will seek information from the Internet. Rather, we will be placing our trust in the professionals who are leading us down this scary path.

Your sweet, sweet comments continue to touch our hearts in a way I have a hard time describing. Thank you so very much for your loving support.

When the girls and I walked into Phil's hospital room, we were amazed to see him looking so well. He was giddy with excitement because he felt so well and because he had seen Dr. Friedman who told him he would probably go home that day. I was just sure Phil had misunderstood him, because it hardly seemed possible that he could leave the hospital one day after having brain surgery! Secretly, I was hoping it wasn't true. I was scared to take Phil home; that meant I was in charge again. When he was moved to his regular room, it wasn't long before Dr. Friedman arrived to discuss next steps for Phil. He confirmed what Phil had said - he would be discharged from the hospital just as soon as they could do an MRI. I voiced my concerns, and Dr. Friedman looked at me and gently asked if I would feel more comfortable spending the night in a hotel across the street from Duke. I got it then, and as soon as Phil had the MRI, we made the trip home to Raleigh. It wasn't long before he was back on the couch, remote in hand, and acting as though nothing had happened.

September 8, 2010 8:30am

Hey everyone, this is Aynsley and Mary Chandler reporting in from Jean Drive. We are both heading home tomorrow (although MC will be commuting for the next few days). Many of you have offered to help with meals, etc. and we are so grateful. Two of our aunts, Lyn Flammia and Donna Flammia, have graciously offered to coordinate these offers. Please feel free to contact them if you wish. Thank you all so very much.

8

IN HIS OWN WORDS

Phil loved hearing from his friends on Caring Bridge. On several occasions, he wrote messages himself to express his gratitude for the warm wishes he was receiving. He would always write out what he wanted to say on a legal pad, and I would enter it on the site. Below is his first entry:

September 8, 2010 9:16am

Ok, and now a message from Phil!

I cannot begin to voice an appropriate response to the show of love and support that almost two thousand of you have voiced through this site. For many people, it would be easy to assume that the messages voiced by Shelly and your responses may simply be the beginning of an invitation to a "Pity Party." I am beginning to understand the words expressed by Lou Gehrig when he said, "Today, I consider myself the luckiest man on the face of this earth." When you take a moment and truly reflect on the totality of what has transpired, and what has been expressed, there is truly much to be thankful for. I do consider myself to be quite lucky today in many ways. I have a loving wife, unwilling to accept my "subtle" changes, which, therefore, led me to seek early analysis by a skillful physician, Dr. Rodger Israel of Wake Internal Medicine. He was unwilling to accept an easy diagnosis and pressed on for the truth. The results of an MRI on September 1st confirmed the diagnosis. He stated that the news was not good, that I had a malignant brain tumor and needed to line up a good neurosurgeon. Not a fun time for him or me, to be sure. But again, due to Shelly's diligence, our very close friend Courtney Ryon had been kept in the loop all day. She had already lined up an appointment for me at 2pm on September 3rd with the world renowned neurosurgeon, Dr. Alan Friedman at Duke University Medical Center...the same surgeon and facility selected by Senator Ted Kennedy upon his diagnosis (among many other "celebrities"). Because of Courtney, when Dr. Israel said I needed an appointment with a good neurosurgeon, I simply responded that I already had one set up with the best. No needless delays. We were moving on with the process now, not later, and it is a fact that our early detection may have positive long-term implications.

We met with Dr. Friedman on Friday, September 3rd at 2pm. He recommended surgery, first offering September 13th as a choice. Then, upon reflection, he noticed that Monday the 6th was a holiday, and he was not booked. He said, "If you are anxious, I will be glad to come in on my holiday and do your surgery," which is exactly what he did. Again, this guy is truly world-renowned for his skills and knowledge, and I am just Phil Greer, a guy he just met 15 minutes ago. Pity Party or fortunate? Easy choice there.

Having been a proud employee of the State Employees' Credit Union for over 30 years now, I know full well that we go through life judging whether our glass is half-empty or half-full and often the correct answer is ours to choose. Here at 3:00 am in the morning on my first night home from the hospital, it's an easy answer. My glass is at least half full. Go back and slowly read the messages, look at the photos. I have a lovely and loving wife, two daughters that I could not love and respect any more than I do, a couple of very fine sons-in-law, three wonderful grandchildren, and two more due in February... Aynsley's fourth and Mary Chandler's first (due four days apart). Talk about a half-full glass! I have loving and caring messages from at least five ministers, a number of cousins, nieces and nephews, two sisters, hundreds of SECU employees, and many other friends. If you do not see the glass half full, go read the messages again. Life is said to be full of limitations, most of them self-imposed. I cannot thank you enough for the kind words of love and support you have voiced; please know it has been very much appreciated. I'm blessed, and you are part of the reason I say so. The battle is not over; it will be a tough fight. With your continued support, we'll kick it.

Thanks, Phil

P.S. (I'm wearing that surgical cap to protect my incision, and it is Carolina Blue!)

9

THE POST-OP PERIOD

September 8, 2010 8:28pm

Phil has now been home for 24 hours, and he continues to amaze us! The steroids are taking their toll making resting/sleeping difficult. His appetite has not failed him, and he is savoring the myriad homemade treats people have provided. However, I think the highlight of his day was having his hair washed. Knowing that today was post-op day two and that the nurse had said he could wash his hair on that day, he approached me as I ate breakfast and asked me if I knew what today was! Needless to say, I did not recall it was hair-washing day, but he was so excited it made me feel like we were celebrating something special. When his hair appointment with me was over, we decided he looked like "Squiggy" from Happy Days, but at least he could say he had had his hair washed.

After reading a post by Cam West, Phil was inspired to purchase Reynolds Price's book, <u>A Whole New Life, An Illness and a Healing</u>. He has downloaded it to his iPad and has started to read. The girls and I are also reading the book. Thank you, dear Cam.

In a weak moment this afternoon, Phil convinced me to take him to "Woodcrafters" so that he could start thinking about his next woodworking

was thrilled to get out of the house and to have something else to
out other than my telling him to rest and take his meds.

After spending almost a week in Raleigh, Aynsley will be heading back
to Montgomery tomorrow. She will drop Mary Chandler off in Greensboro
on her way. Our girls have been our anchors this past week. They always
seemed to be one thought ahead of us and made sure we were always on
track. They have run interference for me and have taken on responsibilities
that have freed me to devote all my attention to Phil and his needs. Mary
Chandler will return here tomorrow night and then commute to Greensboro
for work on Friday. She and Scott will be with us this weekend. Scott has
been such a devoted son-in-law, attending to everyone's needs. I cannnot
close without commenting on my other precious son-in-law Cade. He has
remained in Montgomery taking care of their three children (our grand-
children) so that Aynsley could be here with us. Cade, his family, and their
many friends have all rallied to put Aynsley's mind at ease so that she could
give of herself here. Again, thank you just doesn't seem adequate.

To those of you who continue to comment on this site, we thank you. It
allows Phil and me to be connected to those who mean so much to us. We
feel the warmth of your loving thoughts and prayers. You and our faith
sustain us. God has a plan.

As we got to post-op day two, I could hardly finish eating breakfast before Phil was urging me to hurry so we could go wash his
hair. The only way I could reach his head was for him to sit in the
tub while I used a hand-held shower to wash his hair. His incision reached from one ear to the other, and I had to be very careful as I navigated around the staples in his head. It made my legs
weak to look at the tangible proof of Phil's surgery and to think
about Dr. Friedman opening his skull and removing the tumor
from his brain. It was a fleeting thought, however, because I had
other things I needed to address like trying to convince Phil that
he could not do all the things he wanted to do or felt like doing.

He had had brain surgery, but the steroids were giving him energy and a sense of well-being that made him feel that he could do anything. It was exhausting to argue with Phil and say the same things to him over and over again. I was growing weary of being "the enforcer." However, I was taking my job seriously, and I was going to do everything in my power to help Phil recover.

September 9, 2010 7:46pm

We are now at post-op day three, and Phil continues on his road to recovery. We said good-bye to Aynsley and Mary Chandler this morning as they returned to their respective homes. Mary Chandler and Scott returned tonight and will commute back to Greensboro tomorrow for work. They are also planning on spending the weekend in Raleigh, which will be a tremendous comfort to us.

Phil's only complaint continues to be the inability to sleep due to the effects of the steroids. After speaking with Dr. Friedman's nurse clinician, the decision was made to start his steroid taper a little bit quicker than originally planned. The taper, coupled with a sleep medication, should help with the insomnia.

Hair stylists across the country... breathe a sigh of relief...your jobs are secure! Phil has gone from looking like "Squiggy" in Happy Days to Jack Nicholson's character in The Shining! I'm trying, but we still haven't gotten his hair exactly as he wants it. Oh well, tomorrow he said he would like to try a Pat Riley look. I will do my best.

The next leg of our journey begins Tuesday and Wednesday of next week when we return to Duke to meet with the brain tumor team. It's at that time that our team of physicians and other healthcare professionals will advise us as to which protocol would be most appropriate for Phil's treatment. We're both very anxious to move forward.

My biggest challenge right now, besides the hair, is keeping Phil from talking me into taking him back to work. He just feels too darn good!

As another day comes to an end, I am reminded of the words of one of my favorite hymns, Spirit Song.

O let the Son of God enfold you
With His Spirit and His love
Let Him fill your heart and satisfy your soul
O let Him have the things that hold you
And His Spirit like a dove
Will descend upon your life and make you whole

Jesus, O Jesus
Come and fill Your lambs
Jesus, O Jesus
Come and fill Your lambs

O come and sing this song with gladness
As your hearts are filled with joy
Lift your hands in sweet surrender to His name
O give Him all your tears and sadness
Give Him all your years of pain
And you'll enter into life in Jesus' name

May the peace of the Lord be with each of you. Thank you, thank you again for all of your support.

Saying good-bye to Aynsley and Mary Chandler was not an easy task, especially for Phil. They had given their daddy their undivided attention, and Phil knew how helpful they had been. He loved having them at home with us as much as I did. As he kissed and hugged them good-bye, he became very emotional. It was difficult to watch. I just kept patting him and reassuring him that they would return soon. It helped to know that Mary Chandler and Scott would be back that night and would continue to commute to work for the rest of the week. They would also be spending the weekend with us.

I understood how Phil felt. I was not only sad to see our girls leave, but also terrified at the thought of being alone with him and solely responsible for his care. As long as Aynsley and Mary Chandler were with us, I could expect help in making even the most insignificant of decisions. I simply felt as though I could not think for myself. What used to be routine tasks for me, suddenly became monumental and anything but routine. I would wake up in the morning and just go through the motions of the day waiting for Mary Chandler to return to us in the evening.

September 10, 2010 8:16pm

It's now post-op day four and things are status quo. The steroids are still a problem, but we know taking them is a necessary evil. Each day that passes brings Phil one day closer to completing his course. Sleep continues to be a challenge, but again, Phil is hopeful that tonight will be the night that he begins sleeping again.

Phil's mind was taken off his hair today when he learned that I had killed all of the fish in our pond. I've been put on probation and HR has gotten involved. My job of caretaker of the pond is in jeopardy, and charges of involuntary manslaughter are pending. Having several attorneys in the family bodes well for me, and I think I can have the charges reduced. When Phil told me the pond needed more water, I simply added too much water and not enough chemicals.

This afternoon Phil enjoyed an outing with my brother Dayle. He took him to his office for the 10 min he promised me he would stay. They also hopped into a golf cart and toured the front nine of the Lonnie Poole Golf Course at NC State. What a beautiful day to be on the golf course! Afterwards, they went to a pet store to buy more fish to replace the ones that I had killed earlier in the day.

I continue to say "thank you" and those words just do not seem adequate. Your comments and well wishes on this site, the prayers, the cards, the calls, the visits continue to warm our hearts. We gain strength from those we know and those we don't know. There is simply nothing like the human connection, and we are comforted by it. Hold tight to those you love.

Phil was not the only one excited about him leaving the house for an outing with my brother! I was ecstatic to have a couple of hours to myself in my own home! Although Phil was the only one taking steroids, we were all suffering from the effects of the medication. He had started his steroid taper earlier than the doctors had originally planned in hopes that his ability to sleep would return. He was also taking Ambien, but he might as well have been taking a placebo! He could not sleep, but it was not from lack of trying. We have six beds in our home, and when I got up, I realized that Phil had tried to sleep in each one of them! He explained to me that he thought if he could just get comfortable in one of the beds, he would be able to sleep. I was living as a real life character in the book *Goldilocks and the Three Bears*.

At 2:00 am, I heard him in the kitchen. When I yelled down to him to ask what he was doing, he told me he was making an omelet. I was so tired I could not get up and go check on him. I just said a prayer that he would not start a fire, and I went back to sleep. Although I was also worried that he might leave the house, I was simply too exhausted to act on it.

When I awoke the next morning, Phil told me he had done his best sleeping in the bathtub. I just looked at him in disbelief and went on with my morning routine.

The most innocent victim of Phil's bizarre behavior was Molly, our female Cavalier King Charles Spaniel. She wanted to be held by me all day long. She would not eat, and I feared that she was sick. When I took her to the vet, they diagnosed her as suffering from depression and anxiety. My vet went on to explain that they are very sensitive and pick up on the behavior of others in the home. I informed her of our situation, and it simply confirmed the vet's diagnosis. Molly was placed on an antidepressant, and I headed back home hoping that everything would normalize soon. Everyone's circadian rhythms were off, and it was taking a toll on our entire household.

10

MORE WORDS FROM PHIL

September 10, 2010 8:45pm

Another message from Phil...

OK, the response count is now at about 3,500, and you have me in a corner. As much as I would love to do so, I cannot possibly respond to each one individually. I finally got a slight reprieve, and Shelly agreed that I could go to the office for a brief visit on Friday afternoon! It was great!

Your countless messages have all meant so much to me. I only wish others could understand the connections...old girlfriends (or should I say girlfriends of old?), friends from CUs across the US, old high school friends. It goes on and on.

And Cam West, the book is great! Thanks. It brings to mind another story for you that demonstrates the wondrous goodness of people in general. I was able to find it online and downloaded it to my iPad, but Shelly and the girls want a hard copy. They called a few bookstores but could not find it in stock. At one store, the clerk said they did not have it at the store but she had two copies at home and would be pleased to make them available if we couldn't find them elsewhere! Acts of kindness from strangers! Our Alabama friends have always been important, and we appreciate your leading the way with that crew. Who could have ever believed that connection...being married to our son-in-law's Aunt Elizabeth? Thank you for your support!

I remain particularly amazed that some of you have found sufficient restraint to keep from telling stories on me that don't warrant being repeated here. Thanks!

I also know that some of you understand that I need daily infusions of wisdom to get through the day. I heard some who sound as if they have a guarantee of tomorrow. Forget that thought. If you wake up tomorrow and can get vertical, give thanks. It was not promised to you. For those of you working in the credit union industry, give thanks for another day. For over 30 years, I have hit the floor knowing that today I have another chance to make a difference in the life of one of our members. This sentiment was reflected on a card I received today. It said "People will forget what you said, people will forget what you did, but people will never forget how you made them feel." For most of us, we do not need to reflect back too many years to recall an example of those statements. It is totally appropriate to give thanks for working at a credit union and having the opportunity to serve others. There is no better calling unless you can be a world renowned neurosurgeon.

*I look forward to having my 5-yr-old neighbor Tyler help me feed ALL of our new fish!!

11

THE PLAN

September 12, 2010 8:18pm

To the dear people following Phil's progress through our Caring- Bridge site: We continue to draw strength from all of you and your heart-felt messages. We are so grateful. This site seems to just "ooze" comfort, and we find it hard to articulate our feelings. We are simply overwhelmed by your thoughtfulness.

We have had a very uneventful weekend that is leading up to a very eventful week. Tomorrow we are heading to Greensboro to be present for the ultrasound that will tell Mary Chandler and Scott whether they are having a girl or a boy. We're all so excited and just hope the baby cooperates and is positioned correctly so its gender can be identified.

Tuesday is our meeting with the oncologist followed by a second meeting on Wednesday with the brain tumor team. We're just so eager to move forward with the next step of this journey. The fear of the unknown is powerful, and that fear is exacerbated when one feels powerless. However, once we are given a game plan, we will be empowered to execute it! How blessed we are to have you on our team and supporting us all the way!

Romans 8:28 "And we know that in all things God works for the good of those who love him, who have been called according to his purpose."

In addition to the effect the steroids were having on Phil's sleep pattern, he had also become irascible, and that anger was being taken out on me. He would attack me verbally, which was totally out of character for Phil. He seemed to criticize everything that came out of my mouth. At one point, it got so bad that Mary Chandler stepped in and told him to stop it. Although I knew it was the steroids talking, it was very hurtful. I wanted Phil to be grateful for what I was doing for him, and to verbalize it. Instead, he criticized everything I said and did. As awful as it was, Mary Chandler and I would start laughing because it was so out of character for Phil. It was like "Who is this man?" He had gone from thinking I was the most wonderful person in the world to thinking I couldn't do anything right. I prayed that we would get through this challenge sooner than later.

September 13, 2010 8:26pm

We are just tickled PINK over here tonight! Phil and I were privileged to be present for the ultrasound today that enabled Mary Chandler and Scott to learn that they will be welcoming a baby girl in February! It was a nice distraction from our reality to go to Greensboro and be a witness to such wonderful news!! With Aynsley and Cade expecting another little boy, we will be celebrating the best of both worlds in late winter.

The next leg of our journey starts early tomorrow. I liken it to "training camp" for a football team. We have a great team in place! Our coach, Dr. Alan Friedman, has moved Phil from quarterback to "receiver." Our new quarterback is Dr. James Vredenburgh, and we have heard that our offensive line is formidable! We look forward to meeting them tomorrow. Since we are starting our rookie season, we will be familiarizing ourselves with a new playbook so that we can execute the game plan. Boosters, I expect your full support...prayers, prayers, and more prayers!! We will need positive thoughts and words of encouragement! It's going to be a long season, but as the owner and head cheerleader of this team, I will accept nothing short of a WINNING season!

I leave you this evening with these words from the book of Jeremiah:

"Blessed are those who trust in the Lord, whose trust is the Lord. They shall be like a tree planted by water, sending out its roots by the stream. It shall not fear when heat comes, and its leaves shall stay green; in the year of the drought it is not anxious, and it does not cease to bear fruit."

Love,
Shelly

I was thrilled that Scott and Mary Chandler were allowing us the privilege of being with them when the sex of their baby would be revealed. Phil and I headed to Greensboro the morning of September 13th for this exciting time as Mary Chandler had an ultrasound. Scott's mother Betsy was also present. We all waited patiently as the ultrasound technician pointed out the heart, the stomach, the spine, the brain, the kidneys, and every other body part BUT the one we were all eagerly awaiting. A scream of excitement and sheer joy could be heard throughout the office when it was announced that Scott and Mary Chandler would be welcoming a little girl in February!! Cade and Aynsley had found out a week earlier that they were having another little boy. We were thrilled! The sadness and anxiety associated with Phil's circumstances were tempered by the loving expectation of two new members of our family.

As soon as we returned to Raleigh, I went directly to the needlepoint store and chose a stocking for our granddaughter who would be named Louisa Greer Batchelor. (All of my grandchildren have needlepoint stockings stitched by their "GG.") I would come to associate Louisa's stocking with Phil's brain tumor journey as it went everywhere we went. Whenever Phil was being treated, I would wait and work furiously on that stocking.

September 14, 2010 8:16pm

Our day got off to an early start when we began meeting with our Brain Tumor Team at 8:00 this morning. After discussing Phil's diagnosis with neuro-oncologist Dr. Jim Vredenburgh, AKA Dr. "V" and Dr. Emil Lou, neuro-oncology fellow, we had renewed hope for Phil's prognosis. Dr. V explained the different protocols used to treat GBM (glioblastoma multiforme) and suggested two that he was considering for Phil. Further bloodwork will determine exactly which protocol will be followed. Dr. V said he would be calling in the next couple of days to inform us of the final decision. One thing we know for sure is Phil will have 33 radiation treatments, which translates into treatments done Monday through Friday for six weeks. The good thing is he can have his treatments in Raleigh at Duke Raleigh Hospital! Dr. V also advised Phil that he should not consider returning to work until after the course of radiation is complete. Extreme fatigue accompanies radiation therapy, and Dr. V wants Phil to reserve his energy for his treatment. He has also been told that they do not want him to drive until the radiation has been completed. We have an appointment with Dr. Kirkpatrick, radiation oncologist, on Friday, September 24th. Hopefully, radiation will begin the following week. As I said earlier, we will find out later this week the exact protocol Phil will be following, and whether he will receive a vaccine or other medications to accompany his radiation therapy. The doctors emphasized that Phil has a lot going for him: he is physically OK, he has a positive attitude, and Dr. Friedman was able to remove all of the visible tumor. From this point forward, Phil will have MRIs every two months.

After meeting with the oncology team, it was back to see Dr. Friedman for Phil's one week follow-up visit. When Dr. Friedman entered the room, he looked at Phil and said "What are you up to?" to which Phil responded "197 pounds!!" Even Dr. Friedman chuckled at that! He wasn't expecting a statement of weight when he was just asking what Phil had been doing.

Anyway, he said Phil was doing great. He did decide he would wait and take out Phil's staples next Monday. One thing Dr. Friedman stressed was he wanted Phil engaging in an exercise program in the next two weeks! At that point, I looked at Phil, and I think he had an Albert Haynesworth moment! I could just see his mind racing thinking..." I have to get into better condition?" Dr. Friedman said he did not mean exercise like a stroll around the block! Quite the contrary. He wants him to do rigorous exercise. It's back to training camp for Phil, and as scary as it might sound to him, I just might go reactivate his Healthtrax membership!!

The steroid taper continues, and we are all hoping that Phil will again be able to sleep. It seems his best sleep is in the car so I told him I might just put him in the car like I used to do with our girls and start driving him around town to get him to sleep! It's either that or putting him on top of the dryer!!

We go back to Duke tomorrow for what has been described as an "education" day. We will look forward to meeting more of our team and receiving further instructions.

Keep praying and cheering! Our season opener is coming up, and we want to be ready for the challenge! Our opponent will never change; we will go up against the same foe over and over again until we defeat this disease for good. As always, we are so very grateful for all of the sweet, caring comments that have been posted to this site. I wish I could call each of you by name and thank you individually. To be perfectly honest, I have not met most of you; however, that does not diminish the way all of your comments make me feel or the gratitude I have for your thoughtfulness. Phil is touched as well by the countless good wishes you have sent his way. We are so blessed and so grateful.

Proverbs 3:5-6 "Trust in the Lord with all your heart and lean not on your own understanding; In all your ways, acknowledge him and he will make your paths straight."

Love,
Shelly

We were exhausted after a long day at Duke meeting Phil's healthcare team and learning about his treatment protocol. But we returned to Raleigh filled with hope and excitement, ready to begin the next phase of Phil's treatment. I was like a sponge soaking up every bit of information the brain tumor team was sharing with us. I was convinced that Phil was going to begin his radiation and chemotherapy protocol and respond favorably. I believed that after he completed his 33 weeks of initial therapy, life as we knew it would get back to normal. The brain tumor team did an incredible job of filling us with confidence and hope, which is as it should be.

And yet, never had I felt more vulnerable. Phil's life was in the hands of those who were treating him. It was imperative that they gain our trust, and they did. It was explained that it was either 0% or 100% when it came to treating brain tumors such as Phil's. Either the treatment worked, or it did not. If one treatment did not work, the team of medical professionals would try another. There was always something that could be done. Hearing this served to boost our confidence that Phil would recover.

12

PRESTON ROBERT TISCH
BRAIN TUMOR CENTER
ORIENTATION

September 15, 2010 8:52pm

It's hard to believe that it has been two weeks since we learned of Phil's diagnosis. Things have moved so fast it's been difficult to process everything that has happened. To recap... we learned of Phil's diagnosis on September 1st. He saw Dr. Friedman two days later on September 3rd and had surgery on Monday September 6th! He was discharged the evening of the following day. We had our first appointment with the brain tumor team and the oncologist on Tuesday, September 14th, and met today with other members of the team to complete the first leg of the orientation process. Until now, I have not mentioned the catalyst behind this whirlwind of activity. Courtney Ryon, my best friend, works at Duke University Medical Center as a patient advocate, and she is the reason we are where we are at this point. Our love for her is without measure. As agonizingly stressful and heartbreaking as this diagnosis has been for us, Courtney has been by our sides every step of the way ensuring our every need has been met. I honestly don't know what we would have done without her attention and guidance, shepherding us through every step of the process. She has truly been our guardian angel.

After meeting with the rest of the team today, Phil and I made the decision to have all of his radiation treatments at Duke. Although having his treatments in Raleigh would be a bit more convenient, it would necessitate choosing an oncologist in Raleigh as well as seeing Dr. V at Duke. We decided we wanted to keep it "simple" and have one team, one oncologist, and one treatment facility. Hopefully, the radiation will start the week of September 27th!

Following the suggestion of Dr. V to take his evening dose of steroids late in the afternoon rather than so close to bedtime and the addition of a new sleep medication, Phil is feeling like Rip Van Winkle today!! We think he slept about five hours last night, which is more than he has slept for the past two weeks! I was so relieved that I did not have to drive him around Raleigh all night so he could sleep!! The steroid taper should be complete by Friday; however it is complicated by the fact that our dog, Tapper, is also on steroids, and he is tapering as well. I have to be careful to keep their medications and tapers separate for fear of giving Phil Tapper's and Tapper Phil's. I have had to write both of their regimens down on my calendar to try and keep it all straight!!

After our appointment at Duke today, we came home, ran a few errands, and then left for the beach! I have another good friend, Becky Rickman, who would always say when we crossed over the bridge to Wrightsville Beach that we needed to leave our cares behind, enjoy our time at the beach, and pick those cares back up as we crossed the bridge to go back home. That is exactly what we have done! For the next four days, we are going to forget about brain tumors, steroids, radiation treatments, hairdos and all the other things that have held us captive for the past two weeks. We are going to breathe in the wonderful salt air, walk on the beach, watch the sandpipers run from the incoming tide, pick up shells, rock on our porch, listen to the sounds of gulls and buoys, and count the deer in our yard. All too soon the realities of life will be right back where we left them, but with your continued prayers and support and our personal faith, we will move forward.

Love.
Shelly

Psalm 56:3 "When I am afraid, I will trust in you."

Our day started early as we continued the orientation process in the Preston Robert Tisch Brain Tumor Center at Duke University Hospital. Our first appointment was with Dorothea, a nurse educator, who explained Phil's care and treatment schedule, potential side effects and complications and their management, the ordering and delivery of chemotherapy, and Duke contact information. Phil also signed page after page giving permission to enroll him in a research study that was designed to attempt to develop new and clinically effective cancer vaccines to help patients with malignant gliomas. It would require undergoing leukapheresis, which is the removal of white blood cells from his blood and would take about two hours. I was so proud of Phil for agreeing to participate in the study, in hopes of helping others. Dorothea was to be our contact person throughout the first phase of Phil's treatment. Once it was confirmed that Phil would be enrolled in a clinical trial, all medications associated with it would be dispersed through the Brain Tumor Center. The more I heard, the more determined I was to get started on Phil's road to recovery! I had a notebook that I carried with me so that I could write down everything I heard. Although we were given handouts, I did not want to miss the slightest detail that may be spoken and not included on a printed sheet of paper.

As a very task oriented person, a plan was music to my ears, and I was ready to implement it! I was determined to carry out every detail with extreme precision! I took on the challenge of orchestrating the plan at home while the medical staff at Duke did their part when we were there. I was convinced Phil Greer was going to conquer this threat to our lives.

After completing the orientation process, we decided to spend the next four days at the beach. How nice it was to escape the reality of our lives and head to the coast to enjoy our home away from home!

September 20, 2010 7:38pm

Well, wouldn't you know it, as we crossed back over the bridge from Emerald Isle to the mainland, all those cares we left behind were there waiting for us! We turned left and headed west on highway 24 on our way to Duke to have Phil's staples removed. Although he did not want to leave the beach, the alternative of my stopping at Office Depot to purchase staple removers did not appeal to him!

We were notified today that Phil will be placed in a study where he will receive standard of care, which is radiation plus Temodar®, an oral chemotherapeutic agent. In addition, he will receive Avastin®, an FDA- approved medication that prevents a tumor from making new blood vessels, thus cutting off its blood supply. Following completion of the radiation treatments, Phil will receive another oral chemotherapeutic agent that is manufactured by GlaxoSmithKline, a company near and dear to my heart, that he will take for the next year. We anticipate finding out more about the study tomorrow when he meets with the clinical trial manager. Before that meeting, Phil will be participating in another study that requires that he undergo leukapheresis, the removal of white blood cells from one's blood. It's about a 2-hour procedure, and I am proud that Phil has volunteered to take part in this study that hopefully will lead to a new and clinically effective cancer vaccine to help patients with malignant gliomas.

One thing I have always enjoyed when riding through the backroads of our state is reading the messages displayed on church marquees. As we drove home today, I saw one that I felt described exactly how we feel. It read "Sometimes the best witness is love." All of you who have visited this site have done so out of "love" for Phil. You have "loved" our family with food, cards, calls, prayers, and good wishes. One could not ask for a better witness. Thank you so very much! We hold tight to our faith and are eager to move forward with the next step of Phil's treatment.

Mark 11:22-24 "Have faith in God. I tell you the truth, if anyone says to this mountain, 'Go, throw yourself into the sea,' and does not doubt in his heart but believes that what he says will happen, it will be done for him. Therefore I tell you, whatever you ask for in prayer, believe that you have received it, and it will be yours."

Love,
Shelly

The more we visited Duke, the more comfortable we became with the facility and the staff. As much as I enjoyed being at the beach, I was anxious to get back to our brain tumor team to be informed about the clinical trial in which Phil would be enrolled. After the protocol was explained to us, I felt like a runner on the starting block! I was ready to hear the sound of the gun so we could begin our sprint! We were informed that the clinical trial manager who we would be meeting with the next day would explain in detail what the study would involve. I could hardly wait!

September 21, 2010 7:12pm
The day got off to an early start with leukapheresis scheduled for 8:30 a.m. at Duke. After dropping Phil at the door, I parked the car and began walking to the Morris Cancer Center to join him. As I walked past oncology

clinic after oncology clinic and studied the faces of the people waiting for treatment, I realized that each of them had his/her own personal story to tell. I also realized that whether they were patients or caretakers, we were all members of a fraternity/sorority that none of us would have ever chosen to rush and much less pledged. Cancer is the common denominator that connects us to one another, and although individual battles are being waged, corporately, we are all fighting on the same team with the same goal...to win the battle against this awful disease.

After leukapheresis, it was back to the Preston Robert Tisch Brain Tumor Center to meet with our clinical research nurse, a member of our "special teams unit." She explained Phil's protocol in more detail and stated that 90% of the people enrolled in the study had positive results. She went on to explain that if Phil happens to be in the 10% of the population that does not respond, we would just try another treatment protocol. The tagline under the name of the Brain Tumor Center reads "at Duke...there is hope."

We have one more member of "special teams," the radiation oncologist, whom we will meet on Friday. Hopefully, he will map out a plan for Phil to be fitted with a special mask and set a time and date for the "kickoff" of Phil's treatment!! Every day we draw closer to the beginning of this very long season. The actual protocol lasts for 14 months!

We continue to be strengthened by your prayers and ask that they continue. We are encouraged by the information we have been given and as my dear friend Nancy Williams said to me, "We may not know what the future holds, but we do know who holds the future." Thanks be to God.

Love,
Shelly

I can't tell you how "pumped" I was after Phil had his leukapheresis! During that 2-hour period, one of the nurses came over and told us about her sister who had been diagnosed with a GBM 2 years earlier and about how well she was doing. Every positive story I heard infused me with more confidence that Phil was going to wage a successful battle against this deadliest of tumors! I envisioned our sharing Phil's success stories with others who were fighting brain cancer. I couldn't wait for Phil to be enrolled in a clinical trial for which he qualified! I loved having a plan of action, and I was eager to begin implementing it!!

In retrospect, I wonder how we were perceived. We were so excited about starting treatment one would have thought we were embarking on a trip of a lifetime. In some regards, I guess we were. We were just naive enough to think that when we reached our destination, we would be able to talk about the fun we had while traveling.

September 24, 2010 10:00pm

Today was the day we completed our special teams roster. We met with Dr. John Kirkpatrick, Phil's radiation oncologist, who explained exactly what would happen during his radiation therapy. We both felt encouraged when Dr. Kirkpatrick announced that Phil's neurological exam was completely normal. He attributed this to the skilled hand of his surgeon, Dr. Alan Friedman. He said if Phil had to have a brain tumor, the location of his was about as good as one could hope for. With the tumor being relatively small and located in the right frontal lobe, Dr. Kirkpatrick expects Phil to tolerate the radiation and concomitant che-motherapy without significant side effects. Phil will return to Duke next Thursday to be fitted for a mask that will serve to immobilize his head during his radiation treatments. Because Phil has always wanted to dress up as "Jason" for Halloween, he was excited to hear that he gets to keep the mask once his treatments are completed. We will find out on Thursday when Phil's radiation treatments will begin.

Since we have no commitments until next Thursday, we headed back down to the beach where we will stay until Wednesday. As I was driving

east on highway 24, about six miles from Beulaville, I saw a church mar-
quee that read "Your Miracle is on the Way." Coincidence? I don't think
so.

> *Love,*
> *Shelly*

Dr. Kirkpatrick was a delight! After meeting with him, we were even more convinced that Phil was going to be OK. He instilled the confidence we needed to prepare ourselves for the radiation segment of Phil's treatment. After meeting with Dr. Kirkpatrick, we were given a tour of the area where Phil would be receiving his treatment. The incredible machines that deliver the life-saving radiation were named the "green" machine, the "blue" machine, etc. Phil was given a card that he was to present each time he arrived for treatment. The information on the card identified which machine he was assigned to and the time he was assigned.

We were told that the machines get behind at times and not to be surprised if this was the case when Phil began his treatment. It was explained that being on time for one's treatment was of utmost importance! After our tour, we were given a parking pass that would allow us access to the parking lot directly outside of radiation oncology. We were able to check another thing off our list as we prepared ourselves for the challenging road ahead.

September 29, 2010 7:22pm

After five days at the beach, we are home in Raleigh ready to make the
trek back to Duke tomorrow. As a reminder, Phil's schedule includes another
MRI and then the construction of the custom fit mask he will wear during
his radiation treatments. We had a message from one of the nurses when we
got home that said he could eat anything he wanted before going to Duke in

the morning. Hearing that news was music to Phil's ears since he is trying to maintain the "Big" in "Big Daddy." We are eager to hear when Phil will be placed on the treatment schedule. Monday will make four weeks since his surgery, which is a prerequisite for starting the Avastin® part of his protocol. The sooner he gets started, the sooner he will complete his treatment.

As you know, one of Phil's biggest challenges since his surgery has been sleeping, and since that was Phil's challenge, it also became a challenge for the rest of the family. Well, I'm happy to report that the circadian rhythm of each of our family members, including the dogs, is almost back to normal. Phil gave up his 2:00 am feeding (he was getting up fixing omelets, cereal and other breakfast foods in the middle of the night) last night and stayed in bed until 6:00 am!! I don't who was the happiest...Phil, me, Molly, or Tapper! Those of you who know Phil well know that sleep has never been a problem for him, especially if there is a couch in the room! We're hoping that last night was the beginning of a new trend.

Again, I must thank each of you who has made a comment on Phil's Caring Bridge site. There is no way to explain the emotion evoked by reading your sweet, sweet comments, well wishes, prayers, and anecdotes. From our experience, I have learned I will never be reticent about expressing my feelings and sharing them with others. I have also learned that it doesn't matter that friendships have been separated by years! How wonderful it has been to hear from people we grew up with, people we went to college with, and all the other special people who are lifting us up. I wish I could hug each of you and tell you to your face: thank you!

As we move from day to day, I am trying to live in the moment and not worry about what lies ahead. In one of the devotions I was reading, I was reminded that of all the creatures in the world, only humans have the ability to anticipate the future. Although I would not trade who I am for anything, sometimes I think it would be easier to be a bug.

Proverbs 3:24 "When you lie down, you will not be afraid. When you lie down, your sleep will be sweet."

Love,
Shelly

It's amazing how being at the coast can allow one to escape the realities of life if just for a few days. The anonymity our beach community provided was refreshing. No one knew what it was we were going through. We could go to Emerald Isle and forget for a few days that we were in a fight for Phil's life!

The one thing that did remind us of what Phil had experienced was the effect the steroids were having on his legs. He found it difficult to navigate the stairs of our house. He would go downstairs once a day and back up once a day. Anything he needed that required going up or down the stairs, I gladly retrieved. We had a nice time together...Phil on the couch as he always was and I sitting on the couch adjacent to him catching up on unread magazines or working on Louisa's needlepoint stocking. It was easy to be fooled into thinking that all was well.

13

A TEMPORARY SETBACK

October 1, 2010 7:25am

I updated Phil's journal two different times last night only to see it disappear into cyberspace! They say the third time is a charm!! (Have you ever wondered who the "they" is??) Anyway, here goes...

After driving through a blinding tropical rain, we arrived on time for Phil's 9:00 appointment with the Radiation Oncology Department. First on the agenda was the construction of Phil's "mask" that he will wear during each radiation treatment.

The process of making the mask involves taking a mesh-like plastic, heating it, and molding it to the person's face. It takes a while to harden, so the patient has to lie perfectly still while it cools and molds to the head. Phil found it to be very relaxing, and he took the opportunity to take a nap... evidence that our old Phil is on the way back! The entire exercise took about an hour. As a reminder, the mask will serve to immobilize Phil's head during his radiation therapy.

After the mask fitting, Phil had another MRI. The radiation oncologist, Dr. Kirkpatrick, will use Phil's pre-surgery MRI, his post-surgery MRI, and this most recent MRI to map a plan for his treatment...our "game plan."

Once Phil's MRI was over, we were informed that his treatments would begin the evening of October 12th at 6:30 pm! Although we were disappointed that we had to wait 12 more days for the "season opener," we were comforted by knowing that Phil was well within the 6-week window to begin his treatment. For someone who likes to be in control of the situation, it has been a test of patience to know we must "wait" to get started; however, it's a reminder to me that there will be no "wildcat" offense, I am not acting as the quarterback, and that I must return to the position I know best...cheerleader! I am picking up my pom poms and will plan on leading the team out of the tunnel the evening of October 12th. I will be reciting the "Serenity Prayer" as I try to remember that I am not in charge!

Until that time, we have a lot to look forward to. The Montgomery crowd (Aynsley, Cade, Mary Weldon, Greer, and Martha) will be here on Thursday, October 7th, and Mary Chandler and Scott will join us on the 8th for a weekend at the beach! Cade will fly home Monday with Mary Weldon and Greer, and Aynsley and Martha will stay with us for the remainder of the week. It will be such a comfort to have Aynsley here with us as Phil starts his treatment.

Unless there is a change in plans, I will not be updating Phil's journal page again until treatment begins. With that being said, I am counting on each of you to be standing for the kick-off as our team takes the field the evening of October 12th! It's a prime time game, and we want great ratings!! Plan your tailgate menus and get ready to cheer!! Until then, love to you all. Many, many thanks for your continued prayers and support. You are sustaining us.

Love,
Shelly

God grant me the serenity
to accept the things I cannot change;
courage to change the things I can;

and wisdom to know the difference.
Living one day at a time;
Enjoying one moment at a time;
Accepting hardships as the pathway to peace;
Taking, as He did, this sinful world
as it is, not as I would have it;
Trusting that He will make all things right
if I surrender to His Will;
That I may be reasonably happy in this life
and supremely happy with Him
Forever in the next.
Amen.

You know, when your life is spinning out of control, you tend to look for ways of controlling the simplest of things. Although there was nothing I could control about Phil's disease, his treatment, or his treatment schedule, I could control the activities of our household. Since we would have our entire family together at the beach, I decided it would be the perfect time to have a family picture made. I could just hear the groans that would be emanating from the mouths of my family when I informed them of my plan. It suddenly brought back memories of every Christmas picture we had taken for the past 30 years.

Before informing everyone of my plan, I booked a photographer, decided on the apparel choice, and thought about when and where we would stage this event. I crafted an e-mail that detailed my plan of action, and I sent it out. I let both families know that we would be taking a professional family picture on the beach about 30 minutes before sunset and that I wanted everyone to be wearing blue jeans and a white top. To my surprise, I didn't receive much flack from anyone, and after thinking about it, I realized that everyone understood the importance of this photograph.

We had so much fun that weekend when everyone was together on Emerald Isle, and when the time came for our family picture, everyone cooperated. To the family's relief, I killed two birds with 1 stone that afternoon. The picture we chose, also served as our Christmas card picture that year! I treasure that photograph! It resides on my kitchen island, and serves as a reminder of a wonderful weekend escape when we all were able to forget about the gravity of Phil's situation.

October 11, 2010 6:58pm

Friends and family, unfortunately, we have had a temporary setback. We were informed late this afternoon that Phil's season opener has been postponed. Last Wednesday, Phil noticed a tender spot on his incision, and by Thursday morning, it was evident that he had developed a wound infection. After seeing Dr. Friedman late that afternoon, a broad spectrum antibiotic was prescribed while we awaited the final culture results. By Friday morning, the culture indicated that whatever was growing was not sensitive to the antibiotic Phil was taking. A new antibiotic was prescribed, and we were hopeful that the infection would be brought under control. Unfortunately, that was not to be, and we found ourselves back at Duke this morning. It was explained that the lab was still unsure about the identification of the organism causing Phil's infection and that a decision would be made later in the day about his scheduled radiation treatments. Everything was dependent on the sensitivity report from the lab, and that news was delivered late this afternoon. Although the microbiology lab was still unsure of the exact identification of the bacterial culprit, they were sure of one thing: Phil needed a different antibiotic for effective treatment of his infection. We were also given the news that the start of Phil's radiation and chemotherapy would be delayed until further notice.

There can be no sign of any infection when the treatment begins because of the effect the radiation and chemotherapy have on the immune system. As disappointed as we both are, we agreed that this infection is totally beyond our control and that we cannot afford to waste energy on a situation we cannot change. We are moving forward, hopeful that the third antibiotic is the charm.

As I said at the start of my update, this is a temporary setback. Phil will be placed on the injured reserve list and will look forward to being back in the game soon. We are strengthened by your prayers and are so grateful for all our friends and family.

Psalm 112:7 "He will have no fear of bad news; his heart is steadfast, trusting in the Lord."

Love,
Shelly

As Phil and I rocked on the front porch of our beach house, he happened to mention to me that he had noticed a sore spot on his incision. I immediately took a look and didn't see any sign of infection. I tried to reassure Phil telling him that it was probably just incisional pain all the while worrying that he had something developing under his skin. I checked the spot often, and that night, I applied antibiotic ointment just in case there was an opening we could not see. The next morning the spot was a little bit red, but it did not look much different than it had the day before. However, by lunchtime, signs of infection became evident.

I immediately called Dr. Friedman's office and let them know what was going on. They advised me to bring Phil to Duke immediately. I explained that I was in Emerald Isle, approximately three hours away. They said if I could get Phil there by 5:00, they would see him. I have never moved so fast! I threw things in bags, loaded Phil and the dogs in the car and took off towards Durham. I drove like a bat out of hell all the way down rural highway 24 until I reached the interstate! Once on I-40, I increased my speed more.

As I drove, I crafted my excuse in my mind that I would tell the police officer when I got pulled over. My car must have been surrounded by guardian angels, because there is no reason I should not have been ticketed. I had called ahead and spoken to Courtney. She agreed to meet me and take care of the dogs while Phil was seen in the clinic.

I swung into the circle in front of the hospital at 4:55! Courtney met me as planned, and Phil and I made our way to the neurosurgery clinic. He was taken back almost immediately where Susan, Dr. Friedman's nurse, took a look at him. She cultured the wound and wrote him a prescription for an antibiotic.

By the time we left the clinic, I could hardly walk. I was emotionally and physically exhausted. All I could think about was the clinical trial and the protocol that dictated Phil's ability to participate. To qualify, he had to be able to start the trial within six weeks of his surgery. I was convinced that being in this trial was going to save his life! Now that six week window was being threatened, and I was already trying to formulate a back-up plan. I was going over and over in my mind whom I would need to call and how to explore other options.

As I drove back to Raleigh, Phil and I hardly spoke. I was deep in thought, convinced I had to have a back-up plan. I had to find another way to save Phil if his infection precluded his participation in the trial in which he was enrolled. As ridiculous as it sounds to me now, I thought Phil was going to be that breakthrough patient who responded favorably to the combination of drugs and radiation that were part of the protocol. He would be that patient who would survive! It's amazing how one's objectivity is clouded by total, unadulterated fear! I was like a woman possessed. As we got closer and closer to home, I realized that I had to calm down. I might be worrying about something that would never happen. Phil just might get better in time to begin the trial. I had to cling to that possibility.

After two days of waiting to receive sensitivity results from the lab and not seeing any improvement in Phil's wound infection, we found ourselves back over at Duke where we saw Dr. Friedman. He examined the wound, took another culture, and changed Phil's antibiotic. As I began to ask questions about his readiness to start radiation, Temodar®, and Avastin®, all part of the clinical trial, Dr. Friedman said that Phil wasn't starting anything until his infection was completely gone. I made the mistake of trying to further our conversation with "what ifs." Dr. Friedman immediately cut me off and in a raised voice said "No treatment until all signs of infection are gone!" With that, we were ushered out of the room.

After finally receiving the culture results and sensitivity report, Phil's antibiotic was changed once again to one that would be effective in treating whatever had infected his incision. Although the culprit had still not been identified, the appropriate drug to treat the infection had been. My frustration level was at an all time high. All I could hear was the clock ticking!! The 6-week postoperative period was drawing near.

October 12, 2010 6:57pm

Good news! Our season opener has been rescheduled for Monday, October 18th, and Phil should be ready to go. We received confirmation this afternoon that the antibiotic he is currently taking is effective in treating the organism responsible for his infection. In order to meet the criteria for the treatment protocol in which Phil is enrolled, radiation and chemotherapy must begin within six weeks of removal of the tumor. Monday will make six weeks since Phil's surgery, so he is making the date with no room to spare. He is encouraged to be moving forward. It's so much easier to cope with a situation when there is a plan. For about 18 hours, we didn't have a plan, and we were feeling rather disjointed. But now that Phil can "work out" (and I use those words loosely) with the team again, the confidence has returned, and he is prepared to play both offense and defense. I have to remind him, however, that a bag of pork rinds and a package of beef jerky do not constitute an acceptable pre-game meal!

We are fortunate to have our daughter Aynsley and our youngest grandchild Martha staying with us this week. It's been a wonderful diversion for us, not to mention fun!

Once again, I must thank you all for supporting us as we wait for Phil's next step in his journey. Unless the situation changes, I will not update the journal again until next week.

Matthew 7:7 "Ask and it will be given to you; seek and you will find; knock and the door will be opened to you."

Love,
Shelly

Again, I had worried myself sick about something that never happened. I was so ready to get Phil started on his "road to recovery." I was counting on the treatment protocol outlined by the clinical trial as the means by which his life would be saved. Had Phil not been able to begin his treatment when he did, I don't know what I would have done. I was placing all my hope in in what I considered the "big 3" - radiation, Avastin®, and Temodar®. Emotionally, I could not entertain the thought of possible treatment failure!

October 17, 2010 7:05pm

A quick update from the locker room...Phil is doing great and anxious for the season to begin. We don't have any film to review and are simply counting on scouting reports. As you know, we are facing a fierce competitor. We're taking the approach that the best offense is a good defense. With that being said, there are some pre-game "jitters"; however, as I always told our girls, there is not one thing in our lives that any of us has ever done that we didn't have to do for the first time. Once we hit the field and become more familiar with our game plan, our new routine will seem to be just that...routine.

Ephesians 3:20 "Now to him by the power at work within us is able to accomplish abundantly far more than all we can ask or imagine."

Love,
Shelly

Today was my 60th birthday. My neighbor and dear friend Robin and I had already been shopping for a special gift that I would be able to associate with this milestone. Phil was oblivious to all of it. I had found a bracelet that I loved, so I purchased it and told Phil that I had done so and why: that I wanted something special to remember him giving me for my 60th birthday. He just nodded and said OK. I wanted so much for him to be excited by the purchase I had made on his behalf. However, what I was finding out little bits at a time was the Phil I knew had been stolen from me from the moment the tumor had started its invasion of the right frontal lobe of his brain.

Day by day, the brain tumor and his subsequent surgery had robbed Phil of who he was. The right frontal lobe of one's brain controls personality and emotions. My sweet Phil was unable to recognize that he was not the same person I had married 40 years earlier. As hard as it was to accept this fact, I kept hoping that maybe the Phil I knew would emerge on the other side of his treatment protocol.

14

Treatment Begins

October 18, 2010 6:06pm

As Phil readied himself for the start of his season (taking Zofran® at 1:00 and the Temodar® at 2:00), we could hear the shouts of support, and at 3:00 this afternoon, he took to the field! Nothing calms the nerves like the execution of that first play. Since the treatment was Phil's first, it took about an hour rather than the usual 20 minutes. Having the mask closed tightly on his face for 60 minutes made for an uncomfortable time, but knowing it was going to be over soon, Phil said it was bearable. He was told he would probably lose the hair from his incision forward, but it should be temporary. We are 1 play down with 32 to go before the end of the half! We will continue with a 3:00 start time for the rest of this week, move to 5:00 next week, and then back to 3:00 for the duration of his radiation. On Friday, Phil will add the Avastin® infusion to his game plan. He will receive the Avastin® every other week with the final treatment being administered on December 3rd. We are taking it one day at a time knowing that, with each treatment, we are closer to completing the protocol. It is our hope that the chemo, radiation, and Avastin® will be well tolerated and that Phil will sail smoothly through this first part of the 14-month season.

Never have I been more aware of just how lucky we are as I was today while I waited for Phil to complete his treatment. In Radiation Oncology, there is one waiting room that is shared by patients as well as family/ friends/caregivers. As I sat there, I couldn't help but overhear the conversation among a group of people sitting across from me. It soon became evident that they were there in support of one another, all of them patients with no one else accompanying them. They were staying at "Caring House," a home akin to a Ronald McDonald House for adults. One by one, they were called back for treatment and each time, one of the others would shout words of reassurance that they would be waiting for them when they returned. We left before the last one of the group completed her treatment, but all of the others were there waiting for her. Although, on one hand, it was heartbreaking, on the other hand, it was heartwarming. I couldn't help but wonder where they each lived and where their loved ones were. They were obviously strangers brought together by that common denominator, cancer, but they were there to support one another. They are away from the familiar surroundings of family and friends. They don't have the luxury of sleeping in their own beds or eating at their own kitchen tables. We, however, are fortunate enough to live 25 minutes away from a premier medical center that enables us to remain where we are most secure while Phil undergoes his therapy. We have the love, support, and prayers of many friends and family, and we are so very grateful. I would ask that as you pray for us that you would also include a prayer for those dear people I described above.

How trite it seems to say "thank you," but there are just no other words. We are comforted and humbled by the countless acts of kindness and the sweet words of encouragement.

John 14:27 "Peace I leave with you; my peace I give to you. I do not give to you as the world gives. Do not let your hearts be troubled, and do not let them be afraid."

Love,
Shelly

Having looked forward to the start of Phil's treatment, I was unprepared for how I was reacting. The morning of the big day, I found myself very emotional. I was tearful and scared to death.

Of course, I never let on to Phil that I was anything but pumped to get this show on the road. Maybe it was all the build-up and the fact that Phil's being enrolled in a clinical trial had been threatened. We had made it to the next stage of his treatment protocol, and there was no turning back. This was the real deal, and as one of the nurse instructors had told us, the treatment will either work 100%, or we will need to make a change. Phil was being put to the test.

For the next six plus weeks, our lives would be dictated by medication schedules, radiation appointments, and driving back and forth to Duke University Medical Center.

October 19, 2010 6:50pm

All is well. Phil had his second treatment this afternoon without any problems. Two treatments down, 31 to go!

Romans 12:12 "Rejoice in hope, be patient in suffering, and persevere in prayer."

Love,
Shelly

October 20, 2010 5:59pm

Well, the biggest news of the day is it's the last day of Cipro® (antibiotic) for Phil, which translates to: bring on the calcium-fortified foods!!! For 10 long days Phil has not been able to eat ice cream, drink milk, or drink calcium fortified orange juice because of the effect calcium has on Cipro®. It's been tough on him, but he has accepted his plight and is planning on making up for lost time! It's a good thing the grocery store had a BOGO on Edy's!!

Again, our trip to Duke and Phil's radiation treatment were uneventful, and for that we are grateful. To keep you abreast of the countdown, it's three down, 30 to go! At this point, it's been all forward progress with no penalties. We're planning on record breaking gains and nothing but first downs! On Friday we'll be introducing a new defensive plan...an infusion of Avastin®, a monoclonal antibody, that may inhibit new blood vessel formation, which will starve the tumor. Phil will have this infusion every other week throughout his treatment. As we count down the treatments, we continue to try and stay focused on the task at hand and avoid the pitfalls of thinking ahead and about future treatments.

My goodness! How inadequate I feel as I attempt to say thank you to you, our faithful friends and family. We have never felt more loved and cared for. Because of you, your prayers, and support, we are able to get through each day.

Matthew 6:34 "So do not worry about tomorrow, for tomorrow will bring worries of its own. Today's trouble is enough for today."

Love,
Shelly

October 21, 2010 9:15pm

Again, all is well with Phil. He's almost completed one full week of radiation and chemotherapy! Four down, 29 to go! Tomorrow will be a test of endurance as we spend the day at Duke. Phil will have some pretesting before the administration of the Avastin® begins. Following his infusion, we'll head to Radiation Oncology for his last radiation treatment for the week. The healthcare professionals at Duke have been so kind and compassionate and have done their best to make Phil and me both feel at ease. We're sure tomorrow will be no different. The Avastin® infusion is another one of those things Phil has to do for the first time, and then he'll be a pro.

Romans 5:3-5 "...suffering produces endurance, and endurance produces character, and character produces hope, and hope does not disappoint us...."

Love,
Shelly

October 22, 2010 8:40pm

After an entire day at Duke, I was getting fearful that Phil was crossing over to the dark side, but when he had blood drawn, I saw for myself that he is still bleeding "Carolina Blue." What a relief!

In anticipation of Phil's first Avastin® treatment, we arrived at the hospital at 9:00 this morning so he could undergo "pretreatment." Pretreatment involves having one's vital signs taken as well as having an interview with what they call a "mid-level" member of the oncology team. In Phil's case, it was Mary Lou, a nurse practitioner. She was joined by another nurse named Cindy Lu. Immediately our juvenile minds turned to Dr. Seuss's Horton Hears a Who and "Whoville." We all got a good laugh out of "Mary Lou Who" and "Cindy Lu Who."

Anyway, the biggest concern among the team was Phil's recent infection. Because one of the possible side effects of Avastin® is delayed wound healing, they wanted to make sure that Phil's incision was totally healed following his infection. Once there was a consensus that the antibiotics had done their job and that Phil's incision was indeed free of infection and totally healed, he was given the go ahead to have his infusion. Normally the Avastin® can be given over a 30 minute period, but because Phil is enrolled in a clinical trial, the drug must be administered per the protocol.

For the initial infusion, the protocol mandates that the Avastin® be infused over a period of 90 minutes. The 2nd infusion will be infused over 60 minutes, and subsequent infusions over 30 minutes. Thankfully, Phil had no adverse reactions during the administration of the Avastin® and by the time he was finished, it was time for his radiation treatment. He has now had 5 treatments with 28 to go! Each trip to Duke means we're closer to that magic number of 33 treatments!

After a somewhat stressful week of new experiences, we decided to head to the beach following Phil's radiation treatment. We plan on a weekend of reflection and renewal in preparation for another week of Phil's therapy. Please pat yourselves on the back for it is you, our dear friends, family and new friends we have never met, that have lifted us in prayer, sent us positive thoughts, and have truly provided the "wind beneath our wings." We are so blessed and so grateful!

Love,
Shelly

As Phil and I rocked on the front porch of our beach house, he turned to me and said "I'm so happy we bought this house." To me, that said it all. The house in Emerald Isle was equated with peace, tranquility, relaxation, and hope. My dream of having a beach house had been realized, and I was witnessing Phil's transformation of having it become a fulfilled dream of his as well.

"The Beach House," the official name the two couples so creatively gave to our coastal getaway, had fast become a place to which we could runaway and hide. It always amazed me how once we pulled into the driveway on Island Circle, neither one of us felt the same sense of urgency about everything in our lives as we did in Raleigh. We were able to simply live in the moment. The more time we spent there, the more convinced I was that a Divine hand had been involved in leading us to the unanticipated purchase of our sweet beach home.

October 25, 2010 7:05pm
Week 2 of Phil's treatment is well underway. We had been told last week that all of his appointments would be at 3:00 except for this week when

he would go at 5:00. Once we arrived at Duke this afternoon, we were informed that a mistake in scheduling had been made, and that the rest of his appointments would be at 3:00. We're glad to be back on the original schedule so we can avoid rush hour traffic!

Anyway, 6 treatments down, 27 to go! Phil continues to tolerate his treatment very well. He has been troubled by mild headaches, but we were told that as long as they were relieved by Tylenol, the doctors would not be concerned; however, if the headaches persist, it may be an indication of swelling caused by the radiation, and steroids would again be prescribed. Phil would like very much not to go the steroid route again.

As always, Phil and I want to thank ALL of you who are praying for us. We know our strength is not our own.

In closing, I want to share more wisdom from a church marquee: "For every Goliath, there is a stone." Amen.

Love,
Shelly

October 26, 2010 7:22pm
All is well. Seven treatments down, 26 to go!

October 27, 2010 6:01pm
Wow! Twenty five sounds better than 33, and that's where we are now! Phil has made it through 8 treatments, and he is doing great!! He hasn't started feeling any of the fatigue associated with radiation, but we know that will come at some point. Although it should not be debilitating, the last 2 weeks of treatment are supposed to be the worst as far as fatigue goes. Wednesdays are "lab" days, so Phil had more blood drawn after his treatment today. Because of the potential adverse effects the Temodar® can have on both his white count and his platelet count, he will have to have weekly lab work done throughout his time on chemotherapy and radiation. We don't want any "official timeouts" called due to low blood

counts! *Phil's appetite remains good. In fact, he was excited to have the "meal of champions," a bag of pork skins, delivered to him by a friend this afternoon.*

Phil continues to go into work for about 3 hours a day, and he would like to keep that schedule as long as he feels well enough to do so.

I looked up the word "gratitude" in the dictionary, and this is what I found:

gratefulness, thankfulness, thanks, appreciation,

indebtedness, recognition, acknowledgment, credit.

All of these words defining gratitude don't begin to adequately describe the feelings we have for all of you, our faithful friends and family. The acts of kindness continue to come our way, and we accept them with gratitude. Please continue to pray as we know all of our prayers are being heard.

James 5:16 "Therefore confess your sins to one another, and pray for one another, so that you may be healed. The prayer of the righteous is powerful and effective."

Love,
Shelly

October 28, 2010 5:49pm

"Well, you're through 27% of your radiation therapy," the words spoken by Phil's radiation oncologist when he came into the examining room! Yep, that translates to 9 down, 24 treatments to go, and he is doing great! Both his white count and platelet count are stable. He hasn't lost any hair, and he still has energy! We have so very much to be thankful for.

Psalms 6:9 "The Lord has heard my supplication; the Lord accepts my prayer."

Love,
Shelly

October 31, 2010 8:39pm

We continue to move the chains. Phil has completed 10 treatments with 23 remaining!!

It has been a wonderful weekend with the highlight being the Preston Robert Tisch Brain Tumor Advisory Board dinner that Phil and I had the good fortune to attend. During the social hour before the dinner, we were able to meet a number of people with whom we have so much in common. We found they were either currently undergoing treatment or had completed treatment for a brain tumor. Again, we were reminded of how lucky we are to be in such close proximity to Duke. We met a man from Iowa who flies down here once a month for treatment and another from Missouri whose son comes to Duke. The success stories were abundant, and we left with a renewed sense of hope.

As part of the program, Phil was given the opportunity to make a special presentation to Dr. Alan Friedman, the neurosurgeon who removed his tumor. I don't know how many of you all know this, but Phil has become quite a woodcrafter in the past couple of years, and his specialty is wooden bowls. As a gift to Dr. Friedman, Phil turned a beautiful bowl in which he placed the Star of David. I don't know who was more pleased, Dr. Friedman or Phil! As an aside, Phil has come a long way from his "shop" days in middle school. Phil tells the story of how his shop teacher asked that Phil not admit to anyone that he made any of his items in his class!! Oh, how I wish the teacher could see his work now!!

Our new normal is a leisurely drive to Duke every afternoon, and that will continue until December 2nd. We find ourselves looking forward to seeing our "radiation" buddies and getting updates on their progress. It's hard to describe the bond you feel with a complete stranger once you walk through the doors of the sub-basement of a Duke clinic building. There is an unspoken understanding among the people there, and sometimes all that is necessary is a nod and a smile to convey a message of empathy.

As we head into week 3, we again say thank you for your continued prayers and support.

Hebrews 13:2 "Do not neglect to show hospitality to strangers, for by doing that, some have entertained angels without knowing it."

Love,
Shelly

I had never been so proud of Phil as I was as he addressed the group of people who had gathered at the Washington-Duke Inn for the Preston Robert Tisch Brain Tumor Advisory Board Dinner. Long before we had been invited to attend, Phil had decided he was going to make a special bowl for Dr. Friedman. Although he had become quite proficient at making wooden bowls with crosses, Phil wanted to make a bowl for Dr. Friedman that incorporated the Star of David. There is a special bond between a patient and his physician when that physician has literally saved that patient's life or at least extended that patient's life. Once we received an invitation to attend the advisory board dinner, Phil made the decision that it would be the perfect forum to make his special presentation.

After everyone had finished eating, the program began. Various people addressed the group giving scientific updates as well as board news. There were a number of brain tumor patients that were recognized among those attending that night. Finally, it was Phil's turn. He walked to the podium and asked that Dr. Friedman join him. He had painstakingly written a beautiful tribute to Dr. Friedman after which, he presented him with the bowl. Dr. Friedman is a man of few words, and when he received Phil's gift, he seemed astounded and very touched by the sentiment of the bowl and the fact that Phil had hand crafted it. I was thrilled for Phil, as I knew how much time and dedication it had taken turning that bowl. That inanimate object expressed and symbolized emotions that could not be articulated. I feel sure that the bowl took its place on a shelf in Dr. Friedman's office among other treasured gifts from patients he has treated in the past. I like to think that when Dr. Friedman sees that bowl, he remembers the grateful patient whose hands crafted it ever so carefully to ensure that it was just perfect.

November 1, 2010 6:15pm
All is well. Eleven treatments down, 22 to go!

November 2, 2010 8:42pm
Twelve treatments down with 21 left to go = 36% completed = 1/3 of the way there!!! Phil remains well and energized. Tomorrow is his weekly date with the lab, and we're hoping for more good results. Our eyes are focused on the goal line, and we know with every day that passes, we are getting closer. We hear your cheers; we are strengthened by your prayers, and we are so grateful.

1 Corinthians 16:13 "Keep alert, stand firm in your faith, be courageous, be strong."

Love,
Shelly

November 3, 2010 6:35pm

It's hard to believe, but the clock is ticking towards halftime of this first game. Thirteen treatments down with 20 to go! For the next 2 treatments, Phil will be accompanied by friends (Thank you Lou, Dan, and Courtney) as I am going to be out of town. I will be in New York for a long weekend with the girls (our daughter Aynsley, our granddaughter Mary Weldon, Aynsley's mother-in-law, sister-in-law, and niece). Although I am a bit apprehensive about leaving him, Phil will be in good hands with my able bodied assistants; Mary Chandler and Scott will be here for the weekend to keep him company. I will resume my duties next Monday as we start Phil's fourth week of treatment. Please continue to keep him in your prayers. Thanks and hugs to all of you for being so faithful to our cause. We have a peace about us that I know is not of our own power. We are standing strong in our faith.

Hebrews 11:1 "Now faith is the assurance of things hoped for, the conviction of things not seen."

Love,
Shelly

Having the opportunity to go to New York with Aynsley and Mary Weldon was something I could not turn down. Aynsley's mother-in-law, Nicky Armstrong, had planned a fabulous trip that would include her daughter Ashley, granddaughter Maggie, Aynsley, Mary Weldon, and me. I did not want to miss the chance to see New York through the eyes of my granddaughter, but I was uncomfortable with the idea of leaving Phil. When I made the final decision to go, I did so with ambivalence. Friends had been so kind to volunteer to help, so I took them up on their offers and made arrangements for Phil to be taken to Duke for the two radiation treatments for which I wouldn't be present. Once I finalized the plans for Phil's care, I readied myself for the trip.

I had four delightful days in New York City spent with Mary Weldon, Aynsley, and the Armstrong family. We packed a lot into those four days including a visit to the American Girl Doll Store, seeing Mary Poppins on Broadway, ice skating in Central Park, visiting the Eloise Shop in the Plaza Hotel, and 2 visits to FAO Schwartz! The food was fabulous, and the little girls were so cute to watch as they experienced the wonders of New York City. All too soon our vacation was over, and it was time to get back to reality. I was aware of how much this time away had helped me. I was able to clear my mind and concentrate on the importance of staying connected to the other loves of my life. I had focused all my time and energy on Phil and at whose expense? It was essential that I stay connected to my daughters and grandchildren. We were all coping with Phil's illness as best we could, but at times, I think I forgot how much my girls and their families were affected by the circumstances.

As we waited for our respective flights, I left Aynsley and her group earlier than planned and made my way to my gate. I felt myself being overcome by emotion, and I didn't want to reveal that fact to everyone. I had had such a wonderful time, and for 4 days, my mind was taken off of brain tumors, radiation appointments, and medication schedules. I needed to be recharged and that's exactly what happened.

By the time I arrived back in Raleigh, I was equipped to pick up where I had left off in my attempt to do all I could to make Phil well again.

November 8, 2010 6:14pm

The party is over...Nurse Ratched is back in town! While Phil was flying solo, he received more good news as both his white count and platelet count remain within normal limits. With 17 treatments left to go, today marks the start of Phil's fourth week of radiation therapy. He continues to tolerate his medications and radiation well with the only side effect being hair loss in and around the radiation site. The fatigue he has been expecting has not affected him as of yet, so he continues to go into work for about three hours each morning. He also finds peace and pleasure in his workshop, where he is experimenting with some new and different types of wood.

Upon completion of all 33 treatments (December 2nd), Phil's brain will be allowed to "rest" before he has a follow-up MRI. If an MRI is done too close to the time of completion of radiation therapy, it can show a false progression of the tumor, and that's not what we want to see. With that being said, Phil's follow-up MRI is scheduled for the morning of December 21st.

When we were talking with Dr. Friedman at the advisory board dinner, he asked me if I had "PMS" yet. I must have given him a strange look as he quickly responded... "Pre-MRI syndrome." For the record, I haven't yet, but I know as we draw closer to the time, I probably will. Until then, we will continue to live our lives one day at a time, trusting that the radiation, chemotherapy, and Avastin® are doing their respective jobs.

As always, thank you for your continued prayers. Each of you who is reading Phil's site is a blessing to us.

Philippians 4:13 "I can do all things through him who strengthens me."

Love,
Shelly

November 9, 2010 8:55pm

Seventeen down with 16 treatments to go! As much as I hate to admit it, we greet that radiation oncology waiting room like an old friend. We know it well now, so the fear and uneasiness it once evoked is gone. The faces are familiar, and we are beginning to say good-bye to those who are reaching that magic number of 33. We're also saying hello to the new faces who are just starting their journey. I wonder if they all have the love and support that we do. Strengthened by your prayers, we are able to greet each day with enthusiasm for being, in Phil's words, "vertical." Oh, how we appreciate all the loving thoughts and good wishes.

Proverbs 12:25 "Anxiety weighs down the human heart, but a good word cheers it up."

Love,
Shelly

November 10, 2010 6:07pm

All is well as Phil completed his 18th treatment. He now has 15 to go!!

It was hard to believe that Phil had made it to the mid-point of the initial treatment plan. All had gone well, and we were following our new routine robotically. Our daily trip to Duke was just one of the things we did each day. As we completed each trip, I put an an "X" on my calendar, a visual reminder that time was passing, and we were getting closer to the end of the first part of his treatment protocol. As was typical for Phil, he did not express any emotion one way or another about what it was he was having to endure. He didn't need to; he had me. Each day he completed a treatment, I reminded him of how fabulous he was doing and how much I admired his indomitable spirit! The only thing missing were the "pom-poms."

November 11, 2010 6:04pm

Nineteen treatments down, 14 to go! We are putting one foot in front of the other as we near the 60% mark...or as Phil likes to put it, 21 more days until Shelly hands back the keys! Driving privileges return once the radiation treatments end, and it is debatable about who will be happier, Phil or me! Not being able to drive has been a challenge at best for him.

Phil will see his radiation oncologist tomorrow for his weekly check. At that time, he'll be given his lab report, and hopefully his counts will have remained within normal limits. Although he is feeling a bit more fatigued, he continues on with his normal daily activities.

Thank you for your unwavering support of Phil and our family. We continue to be humbled and overwhelmed by your kind expressions of love and concern. We are concentrating on being gracious receivers and look forward to "passing it forward" when we have the opportunity to help someone else who is in need of support.

Psalms 37:5 "Commit your way to the Lord; trust in him, and he will act."

Love,
Shelly

November 12, 2010 8:53pm

How do we drive to Duke, let me count the routes...honestly, I'm trying to make these daily treks fun, but car bingo and making a list of license plates from different states just doesn't have the same allure as it once did! However, what IS fun, is knowing that Phil has already completed 20 radiation treatments leaving just 13 to go! He saw the Dr. today and was given the good news that his blood counts remain within normal limits. However, he received the disappointing news that his driving privileges won't return until after his MRI and appointment with the oncologist on December 21st. Dr. Kirkpatrick, the radiation oncologist, said he expected Phil to continue to do well these last 2 1/2 weeks of his therapy, perhaps experiencing a little more fatigue and additional hair loss, but no new side effects. We are trusting that this will indeed be the case.

We are planning on having a fabulous weekend, and we wish the same for all of you, our dear friends and family.

Ecclesiastes 3:1 "For everything there is a season, and a time for every matter under heaven."

Love,
Shelly

November 15, 2010 7:47pm

It's late in the 3rd quarter, and we have set new rushing records! Phil is hanging tough and charging ahead with the goal line in sight. It's 21 down with 12 to go! His hair loss has slowed down, and his energy level is still good! When Phil expressed concern over his hair loss, his "bald" radiation oncologist just smiled and did not offer much sympathy. Please understand that Dr. Kirkpatrick is a great guy, and he told Phil it may grow back once the treatment is over. However, he said if his hair does grow back, it could be curly and possibly a different color. I'm trying to imagine Phil with a "tuft" of curly blond hair on top of his head, and it's just not doing anything for me. Hmmm, I guess we'll just cross that bridge if and when we come to it and be ready for a consultation with a professional hairdresser!

With the start of each day, our hope is renewed. Your prayers are being heard as Phil is doing amazingly well. He is executing the game plan with perfection, and we have every reason to believe that we will be in postseason play on December 21st. Many thanks to all of our prayer warriors!

Jeremiah 32:27 "Behold, I am the Lord, the God of all flesh. Is there anything too hard for me?"

Love,
Shelly

November 16, 2010 7:06pm

All is well. Twenty two treatments down, 11 to go!!

November 17, 2010 9:47pm

Running short pass plays...23 down with 10 left to go!

November 18, 2010 9:24pm

The countdown is on! We're in the single digits now!! Twenty four treatments down with 9 to go, and Phil is doing great! The 4th quarter starts tomorrow, and we are counting on Phil finishing this game without penalties or injuries! Friday marks the last day of his "primary radiation" after which Phil will begin his "boost field" radiation.

Let me explain...primary radiation involves radiating an area that encompasses not only the tumor site itself but also the surrounding margins, a larger circle so to speak. Boost field radiation delivers the same amount of radiation but to a much smaller field, concentrating on the original tumor site.

As I said earlier, Phil is doing so well. His lab work is perfect! Although his white count has remained within normal limits, we had watched it steadily go down each week; however, this week it increased! His platelet count is also remaining stable as is his blood pressure. We are so thankful for how Phil has tolerated his radiation and chemotherapy! I am convinced he has a guardian angel sitting on his shoulder. Thank you so much for your continued prayers as I know they are being acknowledged.

As we begin to see the light at the end of the tunnel, we think about those people who started their treatment around the same time as Phil started his. You can't help but overhear the stories of others as the waiting room fills with patients awaiting a turn with their assigned machine...the blue machine, the green machine, etc. Many days the machines are running behind, which affords more time for conversation and the intimate details of an individual's plight. We have watched people go from independence to total dependence in a matter of weeks, which reinforces the fact that one does not have to look far to see someone in a worse situation than his own.

1 Peter 5:7 "Cast all your anxiety on Him, because He cares for you."

Love,
Shelly

November 21, 2010 1:18pm

Duke Radiation Oncology is an eerie place on Sunday morning, and we witnessed this firsthand when Phil went for his 26th treatment today. Because of the upcoming Thanksgiving holiday, radiation treatments had to be scheduled throughout the weekend to ensure that protocols were not compromised by an interruption of schedules. The usual hustle and bustle of a regular work day were absent, and we found ourselves whispering as though we were on hallowed ground (OK, for you Dukies, it is hallowed ground!). Anyway, as you know, the start of the 4th quarter began on Friday, and the clock continues ticking towards that magic number of 33! Phil actually went all day yesterday without a nap, so the radiation-induced fatigue that we have been expecting has not been an issue for him. However, those of you who know Phil and the relationship he has with the couch, it's hard to say if ANY napping is due to radiation fatigue or just normal behavior!! The bottom line is, he is feeling well and this is a good thing! When I tell him how well he is doing and how good he looks, he says "Shelly, I just can't help it."

Although things are quiet around Duke today, that is not the case around our house. Aynsley, Mary Weldon, Greer, and Martha arrived from Montgomery last night, and they will be spending a week with us. How fun to have all of this activity as it does wonders for the soul and reminds us of what is really important! Phil is especially glad to have another male around the house. As I was "delivering" Phil's orders for the day, e.g., when he needs to eat, when he needs to take his meds, what and how much he needs to drink, etc. our 5-yr-old grandson Greer looked at me and said" GG, why don't you just let Big Daddy do what he wants to do?" Life is good.

Psalm 8:2 "Out of the mouths of babes and infants, you have founded a bulwark because of your foes, to silence the enemy and the avenger."

Love,
Shelly

November 22, 2010 6:35pm

For a while today, it looked as though we were going to be penalized for delay of game; however, as the clock was running down, Phil called time-out, and we did not lose any yardage. We had an unexpected injury this morning. After being awakened at 4:00 am with significant abdominal pain that did not subside, Phil and I headed to Duke Raleigh Hospital ER around 9:00 am. Five hours later he was diagnosed with a kidney stone (or as Greer explained to his daddy, a "skinny stone"), a diagnosis with which he is all too familiar.

Feeling refreshed from a dose of morphine and a bag of fluids, Phil got into the car, and we headed to Durham for his radiation treatment. Translation: he rubbed some dirt on it, was re-taped and returned to the game.

Because of his perseverance, he remains on schedule to complete his radiation therapy on December 2nd, which means just 6 more treatments to go! Although we're still in the midst of play, I know whom I am voting for as MVP.

Phil has shown tremendous courage throughout this game. He has looked beyond himself and has always carried his weight, even playing "injured" at times. Executing the plays as they have been called has been the foundation of his success and the success of the team. He knows who the real coach is and has placed his trust in Him.

Thank you for all of your continued good wishes and prayers. As we enter this Thanksgiving week, we are particularly mindful of the many blessings in our lives, and we are grateful.

Psalm 46:1 "God is our refuge and strength, a very present help in trouble."

Love,
Shelly

Are you kidding me? That's all I could think of as I drove Phil to the emergency room. We were so close to the end of the radiation segment of his protocol, and I did not want anything to interfere with his treatment schedule.

I wasted no time in telling each healthcare professional we encountered that I was very appreciative of all they were doing for

Phil, but we had to be out of the ER in time to make his radiation appointment at Duke. As time ticked by, I became more adamant in my quest to get things rolling so I could get Phil to Durham.

After five hours, a bag of fluids, and a dose of morphine, Phil was finally diagnosed with a kidney stone. As the doctor was explaining the implications of a kidney stone, I was keeping an eye on my watch. I assured the doctor that we were quite familiar with kidney stones as Phil had had numerous episodes before, one involving lithotripsy and that we knew the drill. My main concern was getting Phil checked out of Duke Raleigh and over to big Duke in time for his appointment with the green machine in radiation oncology.

We made it with no time to spare. When Phil was called back for his treatment, I fell into a chair in the waiting room and spent those 30 minutes collecting myself. We drove home in silence, as both of us were exhausted from the day's trials. However, the silence was short-lived. As we walked into our home, we were greeted by three squealing grandchildren who were oblivious to the stresses of the day. Those sweet voices were music to our ears and all we needed to be recharged. The only thing that mattered to them was that their Big Daddy and GG were back home, and we couldn't help but be happy!

15

THE BIG DADDY
THAT COULD!

November 23, 2010 6:30pm

This is the day the Lord hath made; let us rejoice and be glad in it. It has been a pain-free, kidney stone-free, and worry-free day! The goal line is so close that Phil can taste it! Twenty eight treatments down with only 5 to go!! The excitement of the crowd is palpable, and he is energized by your cheers and prayers! Your upbeat messages mean so much to both of us and give us hope!

Matthew 25:27 "And can any of you by worrying add a single hour to your span of life?"

Love,
Shelly

Aynsley and our three grandchildren had come up from Montgomery on Saturday, November 20th, and as we always did, we tried to plan some special activities. Since we had to be in Durham anyway for Phil's radiation appointment at Duke, we thought it would be fun to take Mary Weldon and Greer and ride the train back to Raleigh. They had never been on a real train, and since it would be such a short ride, we felt that Phil would be able to tolerate the outing without difficulty. Being able to do something together with the grandchildren would also normalize things for everyone.

Aynsley drove us to Duke, and while she and the children sat in the car, I accompanied Phil inside and waited for him while he received his treatment. Afterwards, we drove to The Mad Hatter, a restaurant close by, got sugar cookies and a drink, and then headed for the train station a few blocks away. Aynsley dropped the four of us off and then made her way to the train station in Raleigh to wait for our arrival. Phil bought our tickets, and we boarded the train for our 30-minute ride.

It was such fun for all four of us! We talked to the conductor and took pictures as we rolled down the tracks. Just as we anticipated, Aynsley was waiting for us at the train station in Raleigh, ready to pick us up and take us home.

November 28, 2010 4:54pm

It's mighty quiet around here! The remnants of a fun-filled week ... the occasional article of clothing, puzzle piece, and other miscellaneous items that were left behind this morning have been collected. They will be boxed up and mailed back tomorrow to their rightful owners in Montgomery, Alabama.

Phil received his 29th treatment last Wednesday, leaving only four to go! It's hard to believe that six weeks have passed since the start of his radiation therapy and that on Thursday, he will hit that magic number of 33!! He continues to feel well. He has lost some hair from the site of his incision forward, but he has yet to experience the extreme fatigue that has been anticipated. When Phil's time in Radiation Oncology has been completed, it will be bittersweet. We have placed all of our trust in Dr. Kirkpatrick and his nurse Georgie and have looked to them for direction and reassurance.

However, with that being said, it will merely be like changing offensive coordinators, and Phil will go from the Radiation Oncologist back to the Neuro-Oncologist, Dr. Vredenburgh, who will be calling all the plays in the postseason.

As we gear up for this last series of plays, we ask for your continued prayers for Phil and for the physicians who are treating him. We so appreciate all the sweet comments and well wishes. It has made such a difference.

Sirach 38:1-2 "Honor physicians for their services, for the Lord created them; for their gift of healing comes from the Most High, and they are rewarded by the king."

Love,
Shelly

Goodbyes are always hard, and saying goodbye to our sweet children and grandchildren was especially difficult. When we were all together for the Thanksgiving holiday, laughing and playing, it was easy to forget the reality of Phil's situation. I knew the next time we would see Aynsley, Cade, and the grandchildren would be the day after Christmas, just 4 weeks away; however, so much can happen in that length of time, both good and bad, and 4 weeks seemed like an eternity. I was grateful that Mary Chandler and Scott were so close by and that we would be seeing them again soon.

16

THE LIGHT AT THE END
OF THE TUNNEL

November 29, 2010 7:55pm

Phil is pumped!! Thirty treatments down with 3 to go!!! Thanks to a co-worker, he has been re-energized by that snack of champions... more pork rinds, and he is ready for the challenge! Pom poms are in the air and the crowd is on their feet cheering, anxiously awaiting the next 3 plays! As one side of the stadium yells PHIL, the other side answers with GREER!! The excitement is building! Keep those prayerful cheers coming!!

2 Corinthians 12:9 "My grace is sufficient for you, for power is made perfect in weakness."

Love,
Shelly

Our time in Duke's Radiation Oncology Department was about to be over. We had become so accustomed to the ritual of pretreatment medications and being slaves to a clock that I felt as though we would need time to decompress when it was all over. Although the time and effort we had invested in our routine was exhausting, it had become very familiar, and familiarity bred security. We would once again be having to learn a new routine.

December 1, 2010 8:22pm

Tomorrow, December 2nd, marks the day that was circled on our calendar as Phil began his radiation treatments on October 18th! Once he receives his final dose of radiation, we will have driven a total of 1,491.6 miles to and from Duke and spent more than 50 hours with our friends in radiation oncology...only a minor inconvenience when one considers what this treatment protocol means to Phil. With this being said, the Durham fire department has been put on alert as he may be burning his radiation mask in the quad once we leave the sub-basement!

As I was going through some papers this evening, I found a napkin upon which I had scribbled down some words I currently find particularly relevant. I have absolutely no idea who delivered these words or where I was when I wrote them down. If one of you reading this journal entry is the author, thank you.

"You must maintain unwavering faith that you can and will prevail in the end, regardless of the difficulties, and you must confront the brutal facts of your current reality." Phil has done both.

Love,
Shelly

As excited as I was that Phil was about to complete the first leg of his protocol, I was beginning to dread the change in routine. A familiar routine provided security; a new, unfamiliar routine, induced anxiety.

December 2, 2010 7:35pm

Greer credits three "Fs" for successful run - could pork rinds be the new power food?

Durham - *After 6 1/2 weeks of targeted radiation, Phil Greer scored on a long pass from Dr. John Kirkpatrick, ending the regular season with a 33 and 0 record. When asked the key to the team's success, Greer responded "It was the three Fs - Faith, Family, and Friends!" He went on to say "Without the three Fs, we were just another team out there. Those 3 things gave me strength to get through each day and a reason to hope. I only wish other teams could have the same experience that I had." With the exception of a minor wound infection and a kidney stone, Greer completed the season virtually unscathed. He attributes his strong constitution to his diet of pork rinds. Experts agree that further research is needed before other teams adopt the consumption of this delicacy - what some describe as looking like the remains of locusts one can find on the side of a tree. Anyway, dietary experts said if it worked for Greer, studies may be warranted.*

The decision regarding any post-season play will be made on December 21st when Greer returns to Duke for a follow-up MRI and evaluations by both the neurosurgeon and neuro-oncologist. With the success he has enjoyed so far, it is anticipated that post-season play will be realized, and that he will have the opportunity to remain on his protocol for the next year. Details will be released in the coming weeks.

In the meantime, with both his radiation treatments and his first round of chemotherapy completed, Greer is looking forward to a weekend at the beach where he will relax and reflect on the many blessings in his life. He wants to thank all of his fans for standing beside him throughout the regular season. Without you, his yard would have been overgrown, his house would not have been as clean, his spirits would not have remained so high, and he would have had a hard time maintaining his "playing" weight.

Romans 8:24-25 "For in hope we are saved. Now hope that is seen is not hope. For who hopes for what is seen? But if we hope for what we do not see, we wait for it with patience."

Love,
Shelly

By the time Phil completed the first leg of the protocol set before him, it had been almost 3 months since we received the devastating news of his diagnosis. He sailed through the radiation and chemotherapy, and I was riding high. My personal challenge of making Phil healthy again was well under way! As we said so long to our dear friends in Radiation Oncology, we passed out homemade peanut brittle and gave hugs to everyone from the sweet young man that gave us our parking passes to Dr. Kirkpatrick and Georgie. They had all played such pivotal roles in providing comfort and security when we both had felt the most vulnerable.

We walked out the same door we had entered 6 1/2 weeks before and looked forward to having time to regroup before Phil had his next scheduled MRI on December 21st. The importance of that MRI was beyond explanation. It just had to be clear!

17

A Christmas Message From Phil

December 14, 2010 9:28pm

Well, it's Christmas time again, a time to celebrate the greatest gift of all, the birth of our Lord and Savior Jesus Christ. With that gift, comes the promise of eternal salvation and forgiveness for our many sins. As we celebrate the receipt of our gift, we remember the deeds of our family and friends through the giving of presents. It's a joyous time to be thankful.

It may be difficult to imagine being joyously thankful with all that I have experienced since September 1, 2010. There is no doubt that Shelly, Aynsley, Mary Chandler, and I have each experienced a level of stress that is uncommon in our lives, yet we all remain thankful for our many blessings. I had access to the finest surgeon in the country, and my treatments to date have gone quite well with no side effects. We have all received loving support and prayers from family and friends, which is so needed in these times. I continue to believe that I am blessed, and I continue to be inspired by your words of encouragement. I'll find out about my next treatment phase after my MRI on December 21st, and you can expect to hear from Shelly that evening I'm sure. We remain confident that we'll move into the

next phase with the same level of prayer and support you have all so gener-
ously been providing. Thank you to each of you for all you have done.

I hope that each of you experience the true joy of the Christmas season,
and are able to celebrate the gift we were given over 2000 years ago. Thanks
be to God.

Love to all,
Phil

18

GOOD NEWS!

December 21, 2010 9:03 pm

Praise God from whom all blessings flow! As you all know, today was the day that Phil had his first MRI after completing his 6-week course of radiation and chemotherapy. The results from the MRI would be the deciding factor in whether or not Phil would be able to continue on with the second stage of the protocol. Well, I am happy to report that Phil's MRI was totally clear! His neuro-oncologist said it was not often that they see such good results, and that it bodes well for Phil. After receiving such good news, we were instructed on the plan for the next phase of his therapy.

January 7th will be the start date for part 2, and this will last for the next year. His treatment will consist of an Avastin® infusion every other Friday, an increase in Temodar®, the chemotherapeutic drug he has already taken, and the addition of topotecan (Hycamtin®), another chemotherapeutic agent, to the regimen. There will only be 6 days out of the month that he will actually be taking medication; however, on days 21-28 he runs the risk of having very low platelet counts as well as low white counts. He has been encouraged to become diligent about exercise as this will help stimulate his bone marrow to produce good blood cells. Hmmm, this is going to be a tough one for him; however, Phil has promised me he will quit driving down the driveway to get the mail and paper and start walking!!!! Oh, speaking of driving, he has regained that privilege and can now drive himself wherever he needs to go.

As those of you who read this journal know, I am convinced there has been a Divine hand in this entire journey. Before we left for Duke this morning, I read my daily devotional, and I must share part of it with you: "Do not fear your weakness, for it is the stage on which My Power and Glory perform most brilliantly. As you persevere along the path I have prepared for you, depending on My strength to sustain you, expect to see miracles - and you will. Miracles are not always visible to the naked eye, but those who live by faith can see them clearly." Today, I feel as though we saw a miracle.

As I have said so many times before, the words "thank you" seem so trite and inadequate when I try to articulate how grateful Phil and I are to all of you who so faithfully follow our story and offer your prayers and support. We are beyond fortunate when it comes to how we have been loved and cared for by you since all of this started on September 1st. What some would consider insignificant acts or comments, have soothed our souls and calmed our fears. As Christmas nears, we wish for each of you a wonderful holiday filled with family times and fun. In the new year, we wish you good health. And whatever path life takes you down, may the spirit of Christmas go with you.

With much love and appreciation,
Shelly

December 21, 2010 WAS the day I had starred on my calendar as it was the day we would know if Phil's treatment protocol had been successful. An MRI would tell us whether Phil would be moving forward with the next steps of his treatment plan, or if the medical team would be forced to formulate a new plan of action.

As we prepared to make the trip to Durham, I tried to go about my morning routine as if it were just another day. I was always on guard, always hiding my anxiety and unspoken fear. We had a full day ahead: MRI at 9:00, appointment with Dr. V at 12:00, and finally an appointment with Dr. Friedman at 2:30. If all was well, our plan was to have supper and celebrate the good news with Dan and Courtney at the Carolina Club in Chapel Hill.

Phil was moving slowly; a cold was taking its toll. However, he trudged through the day with no complaints. Hearing the news that all was well made it easier to muster the energy to complete his day-long stay at Duke. I was ecstatic! We had gotten through the first phase of the treatment protocol, and it was a success! I felt exhilarated! In my mind we were winning the battle; little did I know we had just begun to fight.

When we left Duke, Phil drove. He had been given driving privileges again, and he was eager to get behind the wheel. So to make sure that Dan and Courtney would not have 2 cars in Chapel Hill, we volunteered to pick Dan up at their house while Courtney drove from work to meet us at the Carolina Club. Again, Phil was behind the wheel. It wasn't long after we left the Ryon's house that I was sorry he was driving.

It was raining and visibility in all of the rush-hour traffic was low. Phil was not staying in his lane well, and once we were on the interstate, he was going about 45 mph, still weaving a bit. It was very difficult not to say anything. One thing was for sure...if we made it to Chapel Hill safely, Phil would not be behind the wheel for the trip back home. We did make it, and I was so excited to be with a brain-healthy Phil and our dear friends, Dan and Courtney. I had imagined this night as being one filled with the usual laughter and fun we always had together. My expectations for the evening proved to be lofty ones, and our supper together was anything but fun. Phil hardly spoke a word.

While Dan, Courtney, and I dined on the signature dishes of the Carolina Club, Phil ate a few bites of a grilled cheese sandwich. Selfishly, I was so disappointed. His respiratory infection had taken its toll, and Phil simply didn't feel well. In retrospect, I think I was seeking normalcy, wanting so badly for everything to be as it was before a brain tumor invaded all of our lives.

We finished our meal together, and then I took the wheel as we drove home in silence. I explained to Phil that his driving had scared me, and that it would be a while before I would feel comfortable riding with him again. In spite of the very positive news we had heard, I felt as though the air had been let out of my balloon. The fact I needed to face was this: we had made it over only one hurdle, and there were many more to come.

Mary Chandler and Scott came for Christmas, and it was their year to stay with us the 3 days they would be in Raleigh. It was great fun as we went about our Christmas traditions with my family: Christmas Eve supper at my brother's house, Christmas Eve Service at 11:00 pm at Hayes Barton United Methodist Church, Christmas morning breakfast and opening gifts at our house, and finally back to my brother's house for a special Christmas supper. As the evening was winding down, it began to snow, and as the snow accumulated, we realized our normal plans of heading south to Alabama the day after Christmas were in jeopardy. The weather won, and we were not able to leave for Montgomery until two days later.

As we traveled to see Aynsley and her family, we simply moved our situation in Raleigh 9 hours south. Phil spent the week on Aynsley's couch hardly interacting with anyone. The grandchildren played around him, and he did his best to interject a few comments every now and then and read the occasional book to Martha. Seven days later we headed home.

I spent most of the 9-hour drive back to Raleigh thinking about our next steps and how our lives would be impacted. Again, not knowing what to expect was my undoing. I had become accustomed to the routine of radiation and Avastin®, and I was determined to do the same with our new plan. I was ready to get going with my challenge and goal of making Phil whole again!!

January 9, 2011 12:58pm

As we begin this new year, we do so with much hope and anticipation. When you heard from me last, Phil had gotten a great report from his MRI that confirmed his qualification for post-season play, otherwise known as "phase 2" of his treatment protocol. January 7th was the first day of play. He will continue to receive an Avastin® infusion every other Friday, and for 6 days out of a 28-day cycle, he will receive oral chemotherapy. On days 1-5, he will be taking an increased dose of Temodar®, the chemotherapeutic drug he took while undergoing radiation therapy. On day 2, he will add topotecan to the regimen and take it for 5 days. For these 6 days out of the month, we will have to be very cognizant of the time Phil eats supper to make sure he takes his chemo at least 3 hrs after his evening meal. He has to take his Zofran® (anti-nausea med) an hour before his chemo. He will continue to have blood work done each week to monitor his platelet count as well as his white blood cell count. His most critical days for low blood counts will be days 21-28 of the cycle.

As a result of the high-dose radiation Phil received, he began losing hair to the point of having a very strange looking pattern of baldness. Therefore, he made the decision last Tuesday to have his head shaved. He looks great! If he had a lollipop in his mouth and said "Who loves ya baby," I would think I was living with Kojak! Anyway, his biggest complaint is a cold head. I got him a great looking toboggan and he is happy.

I will continue to update this site when there is something new to report. Thank you for your concern for Phil and our family. I would ask that you pray that Phil will respond well to the second phase of his treatment protocol. As I have mentioned before, Phil's condition will be monitored via MRI every 2 months. His next one is scheduled for March 1st. With MRIs always looming in the future, I am reminded of verse 11 from Jeremiah 29: "For I know the plans I have for you, declares the Lord, plans to prosper you and not to harm you, plans to give you hope and a future."

Love,
Shelly

I would be lying if I didn't say it was nice to have a month free of treatment schedules. I was growing weary of watching the clock to make sure that Phil took all of his meds at the designated time. As the protocol resumed, the treatment schedule became more complicated, and it was even more important that the correct timing be observed. I found it helpful to write all the details down on paper and keep it with Phil's medication. It was a visual reminder to me to administer the appropriate meds at the appropriate time. Once again we found ourselves crossing off days on a calendar as he began the next phase of the clinical trial.

Since Phil's random pattern baldness could be called anything but attractive, he made the decision to go ahead and have his head shaved. Interestingly enough, he found a barber that was also on chemotherapy who had lost his hair. When Phil walked through the door sporting his new look, I reassured him that he looked great! So many men now make the decision to shave their heads so Phil seemed to just be one of those guys. He certainly didn't look like someone who was sick. How deceiving looks can be.

January 23, 2011 10:49am
Friends and family, as you know, Phil breezed through brain surgery, breezed through 6 weeks of recovery, breezed through radiation and the first round of chemotherapy, and had a clean MRI on December 21st. At that

point, Phil's biggest worry was the altering of the earth's rotation resulting in a change of his zodiac "sign." THEN post-season competition began, and he had to learn a whole new playbook. Once again he felt like he was in his rookie season: one medication taken for days 1-5 in a 28-day cycle and another medication taken on days 2-6 in that same cycle. Eight days into the game, Phil took a late hit! Delayed nausea and vomiting from the chemotherapy plagued him for 5 days. He finally had to drop back and punt. His wonderful trainer, oncology nurse Dorothea, was very sympathetic, and after consulting with the team physician, Dr. Vredenburgh, a new play was drawn up that everyone feels will be successful.

When his next 28-day cycle begins on February 4th, two more anti-emetics will be added to Phil's regimen, one of which is effective against the delayed effects of his chemo. Phil has also had to deal with extreme fatigue, something the doctors kept promising would come, but thought he may have avoided. Although he has no appetite, he needs to get back to the training table as we want him to be able to withstand any unforeseen helmet to helmet hits in the future! At this point, he finds himself having to adjust the notches on his belt.

Through all of this, the only complaint I have heard out of Phil's mouth is the fact that he is cold. That's been an easy fix...the thermostat has moved up, extra blankets have appeared, and Phil is dressing like he is getting ready to go ice fishing on a Minnesota lake. I on the other hand, am sporting a new line of cruise wear! We have the best of both worlds here in the Greer household! Phil continues to go to work, and I admire his fortitude. He is one brave guy!

Although we are facing challenges both as individuals and as a couple, we are determined to stay positive, trusting that God has a plan for our lives. We have so much to look forward to! We are learning and living a new meaning of the word patience. We have 2 new grand babies due in 3 weeks! We're praying for cooperation on both of their parts to make their respective arrivals into this world on days that "Big Daddy" doesn't have treatments scheduled at Duke!

Thank you to all of you who continue to follow Phil's journey. We need your continued prayers. As I compose this update, I am keenly aware that there are many of you who are going through your own challenges. Please join me in reading the 23rd Psalm and be comforted.

Love,
Shelly

The Martin Luther King, Jr. holiday weekend proved to be one of the most trying times since Phil's treatment began. On that Saturday, January 15th, Phil woke up feeling awful. He was both nauseated and exhausted; however, he was determined to go to Wilson, NC to a funeral. The elderly mother of one of his employees had passed away, and he was not going to let anything stop him from going.

As he put on his suit, I begged him not to go. I tried to convince him that people would understand if he didn't go. I was actually crying, but it didn't phase him. Prior to his brain tumor, if I ever cried, Phil couldn't stand it. He knew that if I cried, that meant something was really wrong. On this morning, he could not have cared less if I was upset. His only compromise was agreeing not to drive and to riding with one of his co-workers. As he waited for his ride, he had an episode of vomiting. Again I pleaded with him not to go but to no avail. By the time he left, I was a wreck.

Phil's affect was flat. He wasn't talking. He walked in silence to the car never saying good-bye to me, which was not like Phil at all. I followed him out to the car and went to the driver's side to speak to Sid, the woman with whom he was riding. I quickly explained that Phil was not feeling well and that I had tried in vain to keep him from going. She reassured me that Phil would be in good hands and not to worry. I tried hard to busy myself while he was gone, but found that I was unable to shake my worry and concern. When he finally returned, I walked out to greet him. He passed right by me and went straight into the house. I spoke to Sid who told me Phil had done OK, that he was very quiet, but he had not been sick. I thanked her profusely for taking him, and I retreated to the house.

By the time I walked back inside, Phil had already changed clothes and was lying on the couch. Ten minutes later he was sick again. I felt like everything was spinning out of control. I immediately went to the phone and called the neuro-oncologist on call. In my state of heightened anxiety, I had forgotten that I was supposed to call the brain tumor team and speak to the healthcare professional on call and NOT the neuro-oncologist on call for Duke Hospital. Once I connected with the doctor on call, he told me I could take Phil to the ER if he couldn't stop vomiting. I knew right then that nothing would or could be done until Tuesday when everyone would be back to work. Unless Phil became much, much sicker, there was no way we were going to an emergency room on MLK weekend. Phil wouldn't eat and wouldn't drink. He was sleeping all the time. I was absolutely losing it; I was scared to death. The Zofran® wasn't working like it had in the past. Up until now, I had handled everything with such aplomb. I really felt myself coming unglued with the reality of the situation. All along I had considered myself far too intelligent to enlist the help of a therapist. I could handle all of this on my own. I knew what I needed to do, the coping mechanisms I needed to employ. All of a sudden I realized I had hit a wall.

In the evening of January 15th, I made the decision to seek help for myself in dealing with a situation I knew had the potential of not having a happy ending. On Tuesday, January 18th, not only did I call the Brain Tumor Team and seek help for Phil, I also called to seek help for myself.

My appointment with Dr. Renee Raynor, a neuro-psychologist in the Preston Robert Tisch Brain Tumor Center at Duke, was scheduled for Monday, January 24th. In preparation for my appointment, I composed a history of what I had experienced up until that point. What follows is what I read to Dr. Raynor when I had my first visit:

My life as I knew it ended on Wednesday, September 1, 2010 when my husband Phil was diagnosed with a glioblastoma, the deadliest of all brain tumors. His surgery and subsequent radiation and chemotherapy were successful in that an MRI on December 21, 2010 was clear, meaning there had been no reoccurrence of disease. Despite the positive results, I was consumed by the fear of the unknown.

In September, my worries centered around the initial diagnosis. What did it all mean? Was Phil going to be dead in a matter of months? Was he going to be physically or mentally debilitated or both? Knowing that the right frontal lobe of the brain is responsible for personality, was Phil going to be the same person I had known for the past 44 years? Again, I was consumed by the fear of the unknown.

In October, Phil began his radiation and chemotherapy regimens. He seemed to breeze through the entire process, showing very few side effects. Daily weekday visits to radiation oncology evolved into what seemed like visiting old friends. My 60th birthday came and went with very little fanfare, hardly acknowledged by Phil. At the end of the month, I continued to be consumed by the fear of the unknown.

November was much like October. Phil continued on with his radiation and chemotherapy, still suffering very few side effects, if any - maybe a little hair loss - but none of the debilitating fatigue he was warned about. His blood counts remained normal. He had a minor setback when he suffered from the effects of a kidney stone; but even that didn't keep him from heading to

Duke for his scheduled radiation treatment. We made it through Thanksgiving and another month, yet the fear of the unknown continued to consume me.

December was bittersweet. December 2, 2010 marked the last day of Phil's radiation treatments with the only visible side effect being the loss of additional hair. Phil felt well enough on December 15th that I flew to Montgomery, Alabama for a quick visit with our daughter, son-in-law, and our 3 grandchildren only to return on the 17th to a much different Phil. In the 3 days I was gone, Phil had come down with bronchitis and laryngitis and was clearly not feeling well. After being seen by his personal physician, he was placed on antibiotics and told to rest. On December 21, 2010, he saw Dr. James Vredenburgh (affectionately known as Dr. "V"), his oncologist at Duke, and was informed that his most recent MRI was again "clear." That night we went out to supper with our best friends, Dan and Courtney, to celebrate the good news. Phil hardly said a word, and while the rest of us feasted on delicious meals, he ate 1/2 of a grilled cheese sandwich. The good news regarding the MRI was tempered by the effects of Phil's respiratory illness. Our 40th wedding anniversary was December 19th, and it was one of the saddest days I had had. Phil didn't even acknowledge it. Christmas came and went. We drove to Montgomery, Alabama on the 27th, and Phil spent the entire week we were there lying on the couch, barely interacting with anyone. Watching him just intensified my fear, and once again, I felt consumed.

January 7, 2011 marked the beginning of stage II of the protocol of the clinical trial Phil was participating in. His dose of Temodar® was increased, and Topotecan was added to the regimen. Phil took his medications for the designated 6 days without any problems. On day 7 of his 28-day cycle, the delayed nausea and vomiting set in. It was over the Martin Luther King, Jr. holiday weekend, so I was unable to reach the members of the brain tumor team assigned to Phil. The neuro-oncologist on call was very nice but did not offer a lot of options other than taking Phil to the ER for fluids. All I could think about was the emergency room on MLK weekend. On Tuesday following the 3-day holiday, I was able to reach Phil's brain tumor team and receive lots of reassurance for both of us. Phil was prescribed new medication to treat the delayed emesis, and we both sighed collective sighs of relief. It was after this that I set my intellectual snobbery aside and asked for professional help for myself, for the fear of the unknown has consumed me. I am lost, and I do not have a map.

I loved seeing Dr. Raynor. She validated me and offered a lot of support; however, after traveling to Durham and seeing her in the brain tumor center, I made the decision to seek help elsewhere. The brain tumor center was Phil's place of treatment; I simply could not make it mine.

19

HE'S BACK!

February 13, 2011 5:18pm

I am happy to say that I think Phil is back in the game! The new anti-nausea regimen seems to have worked as Phil is 4 days past the end of his second round of chemotherapy having not experienced the first wave of nausea. This is not to say that he has an appetite; quite the contrary. Although he is not hungry, at least he can eat. If he so much as mentions something he thinks sounds good, I will either prepare it or go get it! The only problem we are having with this system is I find that I am eating for him as well as myself!

March 1st is our next big hurdle..another MRI. Just thinking about it gives me the dreaded "PMS" ... "Pre-MRI Syndrome." Dr. Friedman warned me about this malady but assured me that it was a common occurrence experienced by loved ones of those undergoing treatment. I am trying to put it all into perspective and trust that we will receive the same good news as we did in December. We simply must! There are places to go and people to see! Speaking of those people and places, there are two sweet little babies due to enter the world this week, one in Greensboro, NC and one in Montgomery, Al. We are anxiously awaiting the long-anticipated births of

"Louisa" Greer Batchelor and Philip "Harris" Armstrong. Oh what promise their impending births hold.

Your prayers and support continue to sustain us. Thank you for loving us through this journey.

Love,
Shelly

February 20, 2011 7:33am

Borrowing the words of Charles Dickens, "It was the best of times, it was the worst of times."

We are thrilled to announce the birth of Philip "Harris" Armstrong on Thursday, February 17th in Montgomery, Alabama. He weighed 8 lbs 7 oz and was 21 in long. Harris is well-loved and is busy establishing his presence within the family. We continue to await news out of Greensboro, which we know will be no later than February 25th.

Unfortunately, Phil continues to suffer from debilitating fatigue. Although he manages to get up and go to work each day, he is totally exhausted. In an attempt to help me understand what this feels like and for me to find a solution for him, I find myself constantly asking questions like "Does it feel like you have just played 36 holes of golf?", "Does it feel like you have stayed up for 3 days in a row?", "Does it feel like you have the flu?" The truth of the matter is he can't describe it, and unfortunately and sadly, I can't fix it for him.

When we were at Duke on Friday, it was explained to us that because of the location of Phil's tumor, fatigue and lack of focus and motivation is normal. What needs to happen, just like experimenting with the anti-nausea regimen, is to try and control these symptoms with medication. It starts with taking one medication and then adding or changing the meds as needed. Our personal pharmacy is growing, and now I know what Norm on the sit-com Cheers felt like each time he walked into the bar! When I go to the pharmacy counter in our neighborhood Rite-Aid, I am greeted with

"Mrs. Greer"! Although it is going to be a slow process, I have confidence that better days are ahead and that Phil's extreme fatigue will improve. As luck would have it, while in the cafeteria at Duke on Friday, I ran into Phil's radiation oncologist, who I hadn't seen since early December. I informed him of Phil's problem, and he explained to me that in addition to the actual location of Phil's tumor, anytime you radiate the brain, the chemical structure in the brain is changed. He reassured me that everything I was telling him is absolutely normal and agreed that it is a matter of controlling his symptoms with medication. I truly believe that people are placed in our paths for a reason. Speaking with Dr. Kirkpatrick in the line at Chick-Fil-A on Friday, provided me with 30 sec of comfort that came to me at a very low moment. For me, it was an angel moment. Again, I feel that better days are ahead; it's just going to take time and patience!

Isaiah 40:31 "But those who wait for the Lord shall renew their strength, they shall mount up with wings like eagles, they shall run and not be weary, they shall walk and not faint."

Now, on to something fun for spring!

I just recently decided to participate in the Angels Among Us 5K & Family Fun Walk event on April 30, 2011 in honor of Phil. Why don't you join my team, "Head Over Healing?" The more people we have participating, the merrier, and the better for the Preston Robert Tisch Brain Tumor Center at Duke! The walk is through the Duke Gardens, which should be beautiful at the end of April. I hope to be strolling 1 grand baby, if not 2!

This year, more than 190,000 Americans will be diagnosed with a brain tumor, and your support for this under-funded disease is critical. At Duke, ground-breaking laboratory research is translated into treatments for patients more quickly than anywhere else, and Phil has been the lucky recipient of many of these treatments. Your generosity will give the resources needed to push research efforts at a much faster rate. Your participation in the Angels Among Us 5K & Family Fun Walk will help in the discovery of new treatments, expand patient services, and improve outcomes for patients and families. The money we raise will also go to helping to improve patients' quality of life and finding a cure. We need your support, so please join my team and come have fun walking with us!

Love,
Shelly

Oh what a blessing to hear that Harris Armstrong had arrived and that all was well! As excited as I was to know that both mother and baby were doing well, my excitement was tempered by the fact that I was hearing the news over the phone and receiving photographs over the computer.

It was the first time Phil and I had not been physically present for the birth of one of our grandchildren. Although we knew the plan and were perfectly comfortable with staying in North Carolina to await the birth of Scott and Mary Chandler's first baby, it tugged on my heartstrings that I couldn't be in two places at one time. As I sat at my computer looking at pictures of my new grandson, Phil yelled from the den, "What are you doing in there? Looking at porn?" I didn't know whether to laugh or cry! It was such an inappropriate question and so out of character for Phil. I replied calmly that no, I was NOT looking at porn, but at the beautiful pictures of baby Harris. I went back to the computer and just stared at the screen, not really concentrating on what I was seeing but mulling over my myriad emotions and trying to make sense of my life. Where had my husband gone?!

February 25, 2011 7:47pm
I am happy to announce the birth of grand baby #5, the 2nd in 7 days!! Louisa Greer Batchelor was born at 2:28 am on Thursday, February 24th exactly one week after her cousin, Harris, entered the world. She was

7 lbs 14 oz and measured 21 1/4 in. Everyone is doing great, including "Big Daddy." What a wonderful and loving distraction Louisa has been. Wednesday night/Thursday morning was long, but the promise of a new life made waiting into the wee hours of the morning well worth it!! Louisa has already got the men in her life (her daddy Scott, Granddaddy Scott, and Big Daddy) wrapped around her little finger! She has endeared herself to all those who have seen her, and Mary Chandler and Scott have quickly been initiated into their new roles as parents! What a blessing for our family!

Phil's appetite continues to be nonexistent. I have worked it out with "Tropical Smoothie" to add enough boosters to the peanut butter smoothie (his favorite) to make it almost 1000 calories. I don't even need to state my order. They see me coming and ask if I want the usual. They know I am trying to get as many calories into Phil as I can! I would welcome his past cravings (those disgusting pork rinds) if he would just want to eat something. He doesn't feel sick; he simply does not want to eat. I fear that Phil has gotten into a vicious cycle...he has no energy so he doesn't feel like doing anything to work up an appetite. He doesn't eat so he has no energy to do anything. We have got to break the cycle. Again, it's going to take time.

I find that I continue to eat for Phil in hopes that somehow the food will travel from me to him via osmosis or some other force of nature! If this doesn't change, it won't be long before I will be wearing his jeans and he will be wearing mine! In the meantime, we will continue waking up each morning with the hope that the new day will bring a better appetite and more energy. It's got to happen one day soon. I just keep asking myself...how long does it take to get to "soon"?

Psalm 30:5 "Weeping may linger for the night, but joy comes with the morning."

Love,
Shelly

As soon as we received the call from Greensboro that Mary Chandler was indeed in active labor, Phil and I gathered our long-prepared bags and began the 90-mile trip west. Betsy and Scott Batchelor, Scott's parents, were also on their way. Mary Chandler was admitted to a very large room where we all gathered to be present as she progressed through her labor. We were all so grateful that we were being included in one of the most exciting times of anyone's life...giving birth. It was a very joyous time; we were all giddy with excitement as we awaited the birth of Scott and Mary Chandler's first baby, Scott and Betsy's 3rd grandchild and our 5th grandchild.

The room was full of laughter, and I was so proud of Mary Chandler and Scott for being so relaxed and for allowing us to share in such an intimate time. At times we were downright silly! At one point, Betsy, Scott, Phil and I crammed ourselves into the bathroom to hide as one of the nurses came in the room to check Mary Chandler's progress. Things were moving slowly and we were getting hungry. Scott promised to call us if things started moving faster, so Scott, Betsy, Phil and I left the hospital to grab something to eat.

We ended up at a neighborhood restaurant that offered a varied menu. Phil seemed to be energized and hungry. He immediately decided on Calamari for his supper. As silly as this may sound, I was so excited that he made such a quick decision. My excitement was short lived. Once our food arrived, Phil took one bite of his meal and announced he was finished, that he couldn't eat it. My heart sank. The rest of us finished our meal, and then we all returned to the hospital to resume our wait. At 2:28 am, we were thrilled to welcome a healthy new baby, Louisa Greer Batchelor, into our respective families. It seemed we were almost immediately allowed back to meet this precious child. One thing Phil Greer loved was a baby! He held Louisa and shared in the utter joy she brought to so many. After our initial introduction to her, Betsy, Scott, Phil, and I returned to the waiting room where there was a large picture window that opened into the newborn nursery. It allowed us to watch as the nurses bathed our new little granddaughter and went about the routine of checking her out and performing the necessary procedures on a newborn. As Betsy and I watched every move with great anticipation, Scott and Phil slept. We owned the room in the early hours of the morning. Since the four of us were the only ones there, Phil and Scott made beds by pushing chairs together, and the two of them slept until we woke them to go home. Betsy and Scott drove back to Raleigh, and Phil and I headed to Scott and Mary Chandler's house to spend the rest of the night.

As we had planned, Phil and I spent the next week with Mary Chandler, Scott, and baby Louisa. It was a special time for all of us. As I mentioned earlier, Phil loved a baby; however, after she came home, he made no effort to hold Louisa or really show much interest in her. I took her to him often so he could hold her, and I really thought that would be the catalyst that would spark his desire to be involved. It was heartbreaking for me to watch him. I felt bad for Phil, for Mary Chandler and Scott, and quite frankly for myself.

Spending time with our daughters and their new babies was always seen as a privilege for us and had always been such a joyous time. Attention that should have been focused on Mary Chandler and Scott and Louisa was being redirected to Phil. It was obvious that he wasn't himself. He sat in a chair in their den and got up only when prompted to come to the table for meals. He was simply flat - devoid of any emotion. I felt somewhat to blame for being so disappointed and frustrated with how Phil was acting. I tended to set my expectations for Phil's reactions and behavior too high. I longed for the person I had married, and my girls' father, and my grandchildren's grandfather.

It just so happened that Phil had an appointment at Duke on March 1st, which was during our stay in Greensboro. After making sure Mary Chandler had all she needed, Phil and I left to go to Durham for his clinic appointment and MRI. Each time a patient is seen in the brain tumor clinic, they are asked to complete an activities of daily living questionnaire. It was on this form that one was encouraged to mention any change in his/her condition and how it was affecting their normal activities. Of course each time that Phil completed the form, he checked off everything as being perfectly normal. I decided that I would volunteer to complete the form this time and without any hesitation, he handed it to me.

I wrote down as many details I could remember about Phil's activities or lack there of, his flat affect, his total lack of interest in anything, and his lack of appetite. The nurse practitioner we saw that day picked up on what I had written and immediately addressed the issue with Phil. She explained that because of the location of Phil's tumor (the right frontal lobe) and because of the chemo and radiation he had been receiving, his brain chemistry had changed. She went on to explain that adding an antidepressant to his drug regimen would probably help energize him and make him feel more like "being in the game" so to speak. I felt such a sense of relief that something could be done, and I was placing my hope in Zoloft®! Surely the Phil I knew would reemerge soon.

20

HOPE IN THE FORM
OF A PILL

March 1, 2011 7:50pm

I am happy to report good news...Phil's MRI was again clear! After undergoing the hour-long study, he was seen by his neuro-oncologist, Dr. Vredenburgh. He told Phil that clinically he was doing great, but he wanted to see him getting back to life! Dr. "V" was aware of the extreme fatigue Phil has been battling. He explained that fatigue begets fatigue, and that it was imperative that he get moving and exercise! He said he wanted to hear that Phil was "power walking" laps! He also said he did not want Phil lying around on the sofa; he wants him upright. Drinking a lot of water to ensure that he stays hydrated is also a must to help fight fatigue. Sooo, I will be changing from my cheerleading uniform (a bit tight from the increased eating I have been doing for Phil) to my sweats, and we will be heading back to training camp!! We'll pull out the nalgene water bottles and push fluids!! We'll brush the dust off his tennis shoes and have him put on a pedometer! Hopefully, he will be very obedient, and when Dr. V sees Phil again in 2 months, he won't even recognize him!!

Deuteronomy 12:28 "Be careful to obey all these words that I command you today, so that it may go well with you and with your children after you forever, because you will be doing what is good and right in the sight of the Lord your God."

Love,
Shelly

After Phil's appointments at Duke, we drove back to Greensboro where we stayed for the rest of the week. We returned to Raleigh on Friday, washed clothes, repacked our bags, loaded up our dogs and headed south to Montgomery on Saturday morning. We had told Aynsley that Mary Chandler trumped her in that she was having her first baby and Aynsley was having her 4th! We were no less excited as we traveled to meet our new grandson Harris who had been born exactly one week before Louisa.

Phil tolerated the 9-hour drive very well. When we arrived in Montgomery, the excitement around Aynsley and Cade's house was palpable! Children were running everywhere! They couldn't wait to show off their new baby brother! What a contrast in environments. In Greensboro, things were very quiet as we awaited every peep out of Louisa's mouth! In Montgomery, it was utter chaos, and Harris had to work hard to make himself heard! The one thing Harris didn't have to worry about was having someone to pick him up!! Regardless of age, there was always someone ready and willing to hold him.

Phil spent another week on the couch, but there were too many sweet little people demanding his attention to leave him alone to sleep. Instead, he interacted with Mary Weldon, Greer, and Martha from his recumbent position and did quite well. Although he never initiated any activity, he was a willing participant when asked. I was so relieved as the grandchildren didn't understand that Big Daddy was not well. We stayed for a week with the Armstrong family and then returned home to Raleigh to take up where we left off in

Phil's treatment plan. I was beginning to see some positive effects from the Zoloft® and for that, I was grateful.

April 5, 2011 8:33pm

It's hard to believe that it's been a little over a month since I have updated this journal. Over the past several weeks, Phil has been taking a new combination of medications, and what a difference it has made! His doctors explained that his overall energy level could be improved with medication and that it would just take the right combination. Thank goodness it has worked!

Phil has been able to work full days and still stay awake once he arrives back home. His appetite is still not where it needs to be, but I am beginning to recognize a pattern. During the week that he takes chemotherapy, as well as the week afterwards, his appetite is nonexistent; however, the last 2 weeks of the 28-day cycle, he seems to be more interested in eating. It's always a good sign when I hear the ice cream bowl come out of the cabinet, or the pantry door open! That's when I know Phil is actually snacking on his own!

Other familiar sounds are returning to our home: the sound of the riding lawn mower and the humming of lathes and saws. All of these wonderful sounds that I always took for granted are music to my ears now. It's the sound of normalcy more than anything, and I am so grateful for that. I was even excited to see a cigar in Phil's mouth again!

Now, as far as Phil's exercise "plan" goes, it remains in the "planning" stage. Sigh.

I love this time of year as it holds such promise. As we go from season to season, we have the certainty and promise of what each season brings. With that same certainty, I know that Phil is holding his own, continuing on the course that has been laid before him. He is on his 4th round of chemotherapy with 10 more rounds to go. Although it's going to be a long season, I am certain Phil will endure. Thank you for your continued prayers. God is listening.

James 1:2 "Whenever you face trials of any kind, consider it nothing but joy, because you know that the testing of your faith produces endurance."

Love,
Shelly

From the time of Phil's initial brain surgery, every healthcare professional with whom we came in contact emphasized the importance of vigorous exercise! Phil was encouraged from the start to work out, take brisk walks, and engage in challenging physical activity. Each time we left an office visit, I would get on Phil and remind him that he must start complying with what the doctors were asking him to do. He would always respond "I will."

By this time I was really losing patience. It had been 7 months and here Phil sat. I was very vocal with my frustration because after all, I had taken on the challenge of implementing every detail of Phil's treatment plan. I was going to make certain that I did not ignore a single instruction. Although I was not ignoring what Phil was supposed to be doing, he certainly was. One afternoon as I was venting to Aynsley about my frustration over Phil's total lack of interest in making an effort to exercise, she abruptly interrupted me and said "Mom, making Dad walk around the block is NOT going to save his life!" Once again, Aynsley's wisdom surfaced. I was so caught up in what I was supposed to be enforcing and what I thought I could control, that I had lost sight of the bigger picture. She was correct. Exercise was not going to save Phil. From that point on, I dropped the subject.

April 26, 2011 7:46pm

I am happy to report that Phil's successful fight continues! The MRI he had today showed healthy brain tissue! There was no evidence of tumor growth and no evidence of any brain atrophy, which we found out today happens in some people. Although I felt in my heart that Phil was doing well, I was forced to confront my fear of what the MRI might reveal. I always think of Dr. Friedman asking me if I had "PMS," pre-MRI syndrome, and as much as I hate to admit it, today I had a full-blown case. There is nothing better than hearing reassuring news! However, it's like winning a game and knowing that you can relish in the joy of the moment but with the realization that tomorrow you begin strategizing for the next opponent. That's what we're doing.

We are breathing deep sighs of relief knowing full well that tomorrow the fight continues. Phil will begin his 5th course of chemotherapy on Friday, and as always, he will do so with no complaints. He continues to have my admiration. On Saturday, he will join my Angel Team, "Head Over Healing," as we walk through the Duke Gardens to support the Preston Robert Tisch Brain Tumor Center. The tagline for the Brain Tumor Center is "At Duke...there is hope." This has certainly been our experience. Hope sweet hope...that's what it's all about. Thank you for your continued prayers and support. What a blessing you are to us.

Mark 5:36 "Do not fear, only believe."

Love,
Shelly

Angels Among Us Walk

May 3, 2011 8:08pm

On April 30th, our Angel Team "Head Over Healing," participated in the Angels Among Us Family Fun Walk to raise money to support brain tumor research. It was an absolutely beautiful day, and the Duke Gardens were spectacular!!

Our daughters Aynsley and Mary Chandler as well as our son-in-law Scott, ran in the 5K that was held earlier in the morning. They also joined us for the walk strolling our grandchildren Martha (2 1/2), Harris (2 mos), and Louisa (2 mos). Phil's training strategy of holding down the couch served him well. He and the other brain tumor "survivors" lead the teams of walkers as we made our way along the designated route. Phil completed the walk and was waiting for our team when we crossed the finish line. It was a time to mingle with old friends and to make new friends.

It's amazing how the common bond of having a brain tumor brings people together, whether you're the patient, caregiver, family, or friend. The medical professionals, who have become like family to us, were also in attendance. The excitement for the cause and the feeling of hope was palpable. Many, many thanks to each of you who participated in the walk, to those of you who supported our team through monetary contributions, to those of you who were with us in spirit, and to those of you who sustained us with your prayers. The culmination of your efforts helped to raise $1,800,000.00 for brain tumor research!! At Duke there is HOPE!

Romans 15:13 "May the God of hope fill you with all joy and peace in believing, so that you may abound in hope by the power of the Holy Spirit."

With much love and appreciation,
Shelly

June 19, 2011 7:49pm

How quickly the weeks fly by! Can you believe it's almost time for another MRI? June 21st is the day, so I am coming to you, our dear friends and family, and ask that you please continue to pray for my sweet Phil. He has had a great 2 months since his last MRI, and he is now half way through the long season of chemotherapy. If he continues to be tumor free, and if his blood counts remain stable, he will complete the clinical trial in December, and hopefully, the chemotherapy-induced fatigue will begin to resolve! Once Phil's participation in the clinical trial has been completed, MRIs will continue every 2 months, and the Avastin® will be administered every 3 weeks for an additional 12 months.

Since I last updated this journal, Phil has again been placed on the "injured reserve" list. He was diagnosed this week with a torn rotator cuff in his left shoulder. Since there can be no surgical intervention while Phil is on Avastin®, he had to settle for a steroid injection, which should help ease his pain. His orthopedist has cleared him to continue his favorite "isometric exercise" - that of holding down the couch. He has simply had to change sides so that he is lying on his "good" side, the right side. Interestingly enough, the tear in his rotator cuff has not affected his golf swing!

For Memorial Day weekend and the week afterwards, we were fortunate enough to have our girls, our sons-in-law, and our 5 grandchildren at the beach with us. Unfortunately, it was Phil's chemo week so he wasn't feeling his best; however, the antics of 5 grandchildren provided a great distraction, and Phil made it through another round of chemo unscathed.

As soon as we hear the results of the MRI on Tuesday, I will again update Phil's Caring Bridge site. I am only allowing positive thoughts to enter my head. When I do otherwise, it allows the voice of fear to be heard, and I refuse to let that happen.

Philippians 4:6-7 "Do not worry about anything, but in everything by prayer and supplication with thanksgiving let your requests be made known to God. And the peace of God which surpasses all understanding, will guard your hearts and your minds in Christ Jesus."

Love,
Shelly

After experiencing unrelenting pain in his left shoulder, Phil sought help from the orthopedic surgeon who had operated on his right shoulder when he was diagnosed with a torn labrum. He knew that surgery was not an option as long as he was receiving treatment with Avastin®. The doctor diagnosed him with a torn rotator cuff and gave him a shot of steroids. I was at a loss as to how he could have torn his rotator cuff when he literally had done no physical activity to speak of since his initial brain surgery. It was just one more thing to deal with.

Our collective minds were taken off brain tumors, a torn rotator cuff, and all other physical ills when our girls, sons-in-law, and grandchildren joined us at the beach for Memorial Day weekend and the week afterwards. It was wild and crazy as we expected, and we enjoyed every moment. I had planned a week full of themed events, one of which was a "wild west night" where we all wore different color bandanas and cooked over an open fire. Phil loved it as did the grandchildren!

Although Phil spent most of his time lying on our couch, he did manage to accompany us to the Aquarium. He was struggling, and I knew it. He was weak and nauseated, but he was insistent upon going. I am ashamed to say that I was overwrought with myriad emotions. I was excited to be with the grandchildren yet so worried about Phil that I couldn't give my full attention to anyone. I was afraid he would fall or throw up right in the middle of the aquarium. I was forced to move at a snail's pace so Phil wouldn't be left behind. That resulted in our family being spread out all over the aquarium. I was frustrated, torn between wanting so badly to share in the curiosity and excitement the grandchildren were experiencing and sticking close to Phil to ensure his well-being.

As often happened these days, I had set my expectations too high, which resulted in frustration and resentment on my part over Phil's decision to go with us. As soon as I would feel those emotions, it was replaced by guilt and remorse. How dare I feel that way about Phil? At least he was making the effort to be a part of our family outing.

In retrospect, I realized all I wanted was normalcy again. I wanted Phil, "Big Daddy" to our grandchildren, to be the leader of our pack as he had always been. Unfortunately, he was incapable of leading anything. He was a man suffering from the awful effects of chemotherapy, yet he was trying so hard to keep up with the chaos created by 5 precious little children. Who was I to tell him to stay at home and rest just so we could move at a faster pace?

Later that afternoon, we made our way to Morehead City, which is a 20 minute drive from Emerald Isle. Just as we had done with our girls when they were growing up, we wanted to show the grandchildren the charter fishing boats as they came into port with the day's catch. It was always fun to see the big fish that were caught. Phil enjoyed pointing out the big ships that had come into the state port and explaining to Greer how goods are unloaded and delivered to different parts of the state and the country, and then reloaded with goods to be shipped to other parts of the world.

We had an early supper and returned back to Emerald Isle. Although Phil was completely exhausted, he had enjoyed himself. We took some good pictures that bring back fun memories in spite of the difficulties Phil had to work through that day. I had to admire his courage. It would have been so much easier for him to have remained on the couch in our beach house, but he persevered so he could take part in our family outing. What a trooper.

June 21, 2011 7:00pm

Whew! The game plan is the same! No new playbook is needed!! Once again Phil's MRI was as clear as a bell. Our appointment was later in the day than it usually is, and by the time we saw the oncologist, we were the last people in the clinic; however, it was well worth the wait to hear the good news!

After delivering the MRI report, the oncologist went on to explain that a colleague of his is doing an exercise study with people who are receiving

Avastin® as part of their chemotherapy regimen. Well, wouldn't you know it, they asked Phil if he would like to participate in the study. A look of terror crossed his face having heard the "E" word. I quickly joined the conversation and asked for clarification on what they considered "exercise." Before the Dr. could answer me, Phil agreed to be in the study and act as the "baseline." Oh well, at least he is a willing participant.

We are well aware that we have the thoughts and prayers of those of you who read this site. We are also aware of the fact that there are a lot of people we don't even know who pray for Phil and our family. There is strength in numbers, and we appreciate so very much all of the petitions being made on our behalf. As we walked the halls of Duke Medical Center today, I looked up and down the halls and out the windows at all of the activity going on...bulldozers moving dirt at the new cancer center that is being built, patients being dropped off and picked up in the circle driveway, and people staffing the information desks who tirelessly give out the same information to people over and over again all day long every day. I was quickly reminded that regardless of the outcome today, life would go on. As we exited the clinic after Phil's appointment, I felt such a sense of relief for Phil and for all those who love him. We will continue to lead our lives with a sense of immediacy and enjoy every minute of it! Thanks be to God.

2 Corinthians 9:15 "Thanks be to God for his indescribable gift."

Love,
Shelly

One would think that after 9 months of repeat MRIs every 2 months that I would not get as anxious as I did as I waited for the nurse practitioner to give us the results of Phil's latest test. I would always try and read the expression on his/her face as they walked into the room. Had there been changes indicating recurrence of the tumor? If there had been growth, was it large? I had grown quite skilled in hiding my concern about test results. I always

HOPE IN THE FORM OF A PILL

reassured Phil that I was convinced that his MRI would be within normal limits, all the time feeling scared to death as we walked to Clinic 1K. Before any of the routine questions were asked, the nurse practitioner would always go over the MRI results with us. I sighed with relief when we were told that all was well. The usual exam and questions would follow.

First, Phil would be given 3 words and told to remember them... ball, tree, chair. I would always follow along as Phil was asked to perform serial 7s...subtracting 7 from 100...93, 86, 79, 72 and so on. Once he quickly and correctly performed that task, he was asked to spell the word "world" backwards. I would silently spell right along with him...d, l, r, o, w...another task performed correctly. He would then be asked to recall the 3 words he was told to remember at the beginning of the exam. He would always bring his arms up and cross them on his chest, and confidently say "ball, tree, and chair." My heart would finally slow down as he passed another series of mental tests. I dreaded the day when these simple tests would be too challenging for him.

On the appointment days following Phil's MRIs, we would always see the neuro-oncologist as well as our usual cast of health-care professionals. Dr. V was always so upbeat...the eternal optimist, and each time we received good news, we would always leave the clinic so upbeat and ready to go out and tackle the next 2 months before it would be time for another MRI. Who would believe that we would be back at Duke in 15 days with Phil fighting for his life.

21

CAN THIS REALLY
BE HAPPENING?

July 6, 2011 1:25am

We need your fervent prayers!

It's 12:45 am on Wednesday, July 6th, and I am in the Emergency Room at Duke University Medical Center waiting for Phil to be admitted to a room. He will undergo surgery in the morning for removal of a blood clot in his aorta. Let me backtrack and explain how we arrived at this point.

Last Friday afternoon as we headed to the coast for the holiday weekend, Phil began complaining about pain in his left little toe. Neither one of us gave it much thought until it began bothering him during the night. By Saturday afternoon, it was really hurting, so I called the neuro-oncologist on call at Duke. After giving him a detailed history of what was going on, he reassured us that it didn't sound like anything too serious. He encouraged us to continue our beach weekend with the understanding that we would check in with Phil's oncologist on Tuesday, which is what we did.

Per Dr. V's advice, we headed to the ER at Duke Raleigh Hospital. It was there that Phil was diagnosed with a large blood clot in his aorta. Knowing that Phil was being treated at DUMC for his brain tumor, the ER physician arranged for him to be transferred via ambulance to Durham. We met with some of the members of his surgical team, who explained the seriousness of Phil's situation. They told us that one of the complications of having a glioblastoma is the threat of blood clots. This was news to us! No one had ever mentioned blood clots as a potential complication. I was beginning to wonder about all the other potential risks associated with having a GBM! It became evident that we didn't know what we didn't know.

Because of the location of Phil's clot, both his bowels and kidneys are in jeopardy. Another obstacle Phil is facing is having surgery while taking Avastin®. As you may recall, Avastin® works by starving a tumor of it's blood supply. Although that's good news for treating tumors, it's not so good news for the healing process following surgery. As we face the most challenging health crisis since Phil's initial surgery, I ask that you pray for Phil's well-being, that he will come through the surgery without any complications, and that he will heal. I also ask that you pray that his tumor will remain stable, as he will be going off the Avastin®, which we feel has been his life saver. And it goes without saying, please pray for the skilled hands of the surgeons, who will work hard to save Phil's life.

It's hard to believe it has been 10 months since I first started communicating to you, our family and friends via this Caring Bridge site. As I have said each time I make an entry, thank you for all of your loving support. There is no way we could have gotten through these months without you and the kind thoughts, the kind deeds, and the prayers you have said on our behalf. To say I am frightened is an understatement, but I am determined to remain as calm as I can and offer Phil my unwavering love and support. He has remained so strong through every bit of this journey. He has never once complained about having to undergo all of the treatments he has had to endure. He is my hero.

Psalms 28:6-7 "Blessed be the Lord, for he has heard the sound of my pleadings. The Lord is my strength and my shield; in him my heart trusts;

so I am helped, and my heart exults, and with my song, I give thanks to him."

Love,
Shelly

We had great plans for the 4th of July weekend! In order to avoid driving all the way to Durham for Phil's scheduled blood work, he had it done at Duke Raleigh Hospital on Friday morning. We were looking forward to having my brother, sister-in-law, and sister join us for the long holiday weekend. As we began driving to the coast, Phil complained to me that his little toe on his left foot was hurting. I'm going to be honest, all I could think of was...you have got to be kidding me! He had been through so much without a single complaint, and now all he could talk about was his left little toe!!

When we arrived in Emerald Isle, the first thing I did was examine the toe in question. It looked like a normal toe to me! I was ready for Phil to give it up about his toe, but he didn't. It kept him awake throughout the night. By Saturday morning, the toe was beginning to take on a blueish tint and the pain had spread to his 3rd and 4th toes. He continued to take analgesics for his pain, and that gave him some relief. I tried to play it down not only for him, but for me. I didn't want anything to ruin our weekend.

I was sick of Phil being sick. I wanted so badly for him to be healthy again. I wanted a normal weekend for him as much as I wanted it for myself. It was the first time we had extended an invitation to my brother, sister-in-law, and sister to spend a weekend at the beach with us. Oh what fun I had planned on having, and now everything I had looked forward to, was going down the drain. I realized I simply could not make plans anymore without a back-up plan in place. It was imperative that I not set such high expectations when every plan was in jeopardy.

Phil agreed to go to the beach where he sat silently under an umbrella; he didn't last an hour. By Saturday afternoon, I realized I needed to check in with someone at Duke. I called and spoke with the resident on call. After I gave him a detailed history of what was going on, he reassured me that it didn't sound like an emergent situation. He advised that we continue our time at the coast and to check in with Dr. V when we returned to Raleigh.

I tried to reassure Phil, but I knew he was worried. I knew what he was thinking. His father, who had died of lung cancer, had experienced the same symptoms that had eventually led to the amputation of one of his legs. I tried to convince him he didn't have the same thing, but I was worried. Since Phil looked to me for reassurance, I wasn't about to act like I was that concerned. However, my family guests were concerned, and they encouraged me to return home.

When we arrived back in Raleigh, our neighbor, who is an internist, came over and took a look at Phil. Although nothing jumped out at him, he told us that Phil's symptoms were characteristic of a problem higher up than his legs. He also advised that we get in touch with our Duke team the next day. When I was able to talk to the staff the next morning, I was told that there were no appointments available, and that Dr. V recommended that we go to the emergency room. Phil had the presence of mind to direct me to Duke Raleigh Hospital rather than another hospital to which I was headed. Duke Raleigh would have access to his records since he had been treated there previously.

When we arrived at the emergency room, it was so crowded that we had to wait for quite a while only to have Phil placed on a gurney in the hallway once he was finally called back. The ER doctor examined him and didn't find anything that alarmed him. I gave him the names and numbers of our brain tumor team at Duke.

After a phone consultation and at Dr. V's request, the ER physician ordered a CT arteriogram that revealed a very large blood clot in Phil's aorta. At this point, we had been in the emergency room for 9 hours. When the news of Phil's diagnosis was delivered to us, I responded that I would go get the car and take him directly to Duke; however, the ER physician quickly informed me that the only way Phil would be going to Duke was by ambulance. He would need to be closely monitored from this point forward. I was beginning to get an idea of the true seriousness of his situation.

My brother had come to check on us and was present when we received the news. It was 11:00 before a critical care ambulance was available to transport Phil. When the ambulance left with him heading to Durham, my brother followed me home. I packed a few things, and Dayle drove me to the Duke ER where I was taken back to be with Phil. The speed with which they were attending to Phil confirmed the seriousness of the situation.

Shortly after I arrived, 2 Italian cardio-thoracic surgeons came in to examine him. They were conversing in Italian for what seemed like an eternity. They finally concurred with each other and then turned their attention to Phil and me. We were informed that Phil was critical and that he would need surgery. He was moved to first in line for surgery the next morning; however, his vital signs would be monitored every 15 minutes throughout the night, and if anything changed, they would take him into surgery immediately. Everything was happening so fast that I was having trouble processing all the details of what I was hearing. I felt like I was going into auto pilot mode and just going through the paces.

I followed Phil as they moved him to a room on a telemetry floor, all the while keeping an upbeat attitude for Phil, trying to reassure him. In the darkness of his room, I suddenly realized that there was a good possibility that I could lose Phil. As he slept, I sat in a chair beside him and cried. All these months I had worried about his GBM and keeping it under control. Now, Phil was staring death in the face, not due to a brain tumor, but rather a blood clot. Why? How could this be? What was going to happen? Was he going to live through the night? Was he going to survive the surgery? By this time, it was 12:30 in the morning.

The hospital staff was in the room at least every 15 minutes if not more often. They were drawing blood, constantly checking Phil's hemoglobin to make sure he was not bleeding internally. I had never felt so alone and so insignificant. I was just an observer in a room of frantic activity. At 5:00 am, the surgeon who would be doing the surgery came in to talk to us and explain the planned course of events.

At this point, I was relieved that Phil had made it through the night and that he would be in surgery soon. Mary Chandler and other family members and friends would be gathering to offer their support. I was exhausted. I felt myself detaching from the situation, just going through the motions and following instructions I was given. As they wheeled Phil out of his room to the surgical suite, I kissed him good-bye not knowing if it would be the last time I saw him alive. I grabbed my personal belongings and made my way to the surgical waiting room.

Unlike Labor Day when Phil had his brain surgery, the scene in the waiting room was vastly different! It was packed with people doing the same thing as I, waiting to hear the outcome of a loved one's surgery. I staked out a corner to sit and begin the long wait. Before I knew it, the little corner I had claimed as my own began filling up with family, friends, and co-workers. Louisa entertained us as only a baby can.

Before I knew it, the receptionist was paging us and directing us to a small conference room where we would be speaking with Dr. Cox, Phil's surgeon. Mary Chandler and I were happy to hear that the surgery had gone well. With that news, we headed home for a shower, a change of clothes and some much needed rest.

July 6, 2011 1:42pm

From Aynsley

Just a quick note to let you know that the surgery went as well as could be expected. My dad has been moved to ICU, and mom and Mary Chandler are headed to see him now. Mom will have a full update later today. Thank you all so much for your prayers. Please continue to pray.

July 7, 2011 7:23am

Phil is very patriotic and loves the 4th of July holiday, but I told him his desperate attempt to find something to complete his red and white outfit cannot include blue toes! Thankfully, those blue toes should be improving and regaining their more normal "pink" color.

As Aynsley communicated in her update yesterday, Phil's surgery went very well. The surgeon (Dr. Cox) said there were no surprises; they simply opened the aorta and removed the clot, looked around, and closed him up. How fortunate for Phil.

It was interesting to hear Dr. Cox say that he had seen only 5 or 6 aortic blood clots in his career. He also said that, for his age, Phil's aorta looked great! It must be Phil's attention to a "healthy" diet and exercise! Needless to say, we were all so relieved.

After surgery, Phil was moved to the intensive care unit, where visiting hours are very strict. Mary Chandler and I were able to see him for a brief period yesterday afternoon. He was still heavily sedated, but it was good just to see him. We went back last night when visiting hours began again at 8:30. Phil was still in a deep sleep and connected to a ventilator. His nurse said if we came back in 30 min, we would see a big difference as they were getting ready to stop his sedation and remove the breathing tube. We did like the nurse said, and when we returned, it was a completely different picture!

As soon as he heard our voices, he opened his eyes and waved to us. His throat was so dry it was difficult for him to speak, but he did manage to say a few words. He winked at Mary Chandler and perked up when we told him that Aynsley and Harris would be flying in today. We were feeling so much better about the entire situation when we left Duke last night!

I have just gotten off the phone with Phil's ICU nurse, and he had a very good night. Dr. Cox and his team have been by, but no one knows yet what the plan is for moving Phil to a step-down unit. His nurse assured me that she would call and let me know the plan as soon as she knows what that plan is. I will be sure to update this site as soon as I know more.

It was a grueling 36 hours and there is no way that we could have gotten through it without the precious love and support of our family and friends. As always, the words "thank you" do not adequately convey our gratitude. Oh, how blessed we are. Until I know more, please continue to pray for our sweet Phil.

Jeremiah 30:17 "For I will restore health to you, and your wounds I will heal, says the Lord."

Love,
Shelly

Everything had moved so fast I was still trying to process what had happened over the course of just a few days. We came so close to losing Phil to what could have been a very horrific, painful death. There were so many "what ifs" that were racing through my mind...What if the blood clot had occluded his mesenteric artery and affected his bowels? What if the blood clot had occluded his renal arteries and affected his kidneys? It went on and on. I had to stop myself because none of that happened.

Now, I was faced with helping Phil recover from a difficult surgery. I was comforted not only by having Mary Chandler by my side, but also the anticipation of Aynsley's arrival. Our two girls stepped up to the plate and ran our household, answered the phone, and helped me make difficult decisions. Their devotion to both Phil and me was the catalyst that kept me going. I had never felt a deeper bond with my daughters.

July 9, 2011 2:13am

Anyone who has spent time in a hospital knows it is not a place of serenity that promotes rest, unless that is, one is heavily medicated. It is 2:15 am, and the sounds of monitoring devices and conversations among the night staff fill the air. Phil is fast asleep, so that's a good thing. He was moved to a step-down floor around 3:00 on Friday afternoon. He has done well for the most part, but the doctors have been concerned about his red blood cell counts. Before leaving the ICU, he received a unit of blood, and he has received 2 more units since being moved. Labs were drawn at 3:15 am, and one of the interns just came in to say that the lab results showed his counts have gone up significantly, which is good news! With Phil having been on Avastin®, bleeding and delayed healing are always a risk.

Phil will have blood drawn every six hours to ensure that his counts remain stable. I will continue to update this site as I receive new information. If you do not hear from me, please consider no news as good news. Please continue to pray for wound healing, both internally and externally. Oh how grateful we are to have such dedicated prayer warriors.

Love,
Shelly

Once Phil was moved to a step-down unit, I was again able to stay with him. I packed the familiar "hospital" bag that included my iPad, needlepoint, magazines, prayer shawl, and my pillow, and claimed my spot on the chair that would be my home for the next week. Being in Phil's room gave me the feeling of "control" that I so badly needed. I was able to minister to him as well as call for reinforcements when I could not meet his needs.

Phil's incision was 13 inches long from the bottom of his sternum to his pubic bone. Moving was very difficult for him. He had to be reminded how to turn over on his side before trying to sit up. I felt so bad for him. He never complained, yet I knew he was hurting. He had a button to push to administer his pain meds, and he pushed it often, but I never heard him say a thing.

Medical students, interns, residents, and attending physicians visited Phil's room often. Morning rounds started between 5:30 am and 6:00 am. Because that was the time to hear the discussion among the physicians and a time to converse with them and ask questions, I was disappointed when I would awake and realize that I had slept through rounds.

July 12, 2011 11:16am

As the song goes, "Boom boom, ain't it great to be crazy," which describes Phil for the past two days. Once it was determined that Phil was suffering from the effects of pain medications and not from any serious complications, we all enjoyed the comic relief that he provided. When he is feeling better, I will share with him his funny commentary.

Phil continues to recover nicely. He does not realize how notorious he has become among the medical community here at Duke. Because blood clots in the aorta are so rare, everyone is interested in his story. His oncology team told us the data reported 0.8% of patients on Avastin® developed arterial clots. With that being said, we remain convinced that the benefits the drug provided in treating Phil's GBM outweighed the potential risks involved. Phil's Avastin® days are probably over, but his oncology team is putting their respective heads together to develop a new plan of action for him. We have been assured that there are many more treatment options out there, and as soon as Phil has had ample time to recover from his surgery, he will again begin aggressive treatment of his brain tumor.

I cannot believe it was just a week ago that Phil's problem was diagnosed. We owe a debt of gratitude to Dr. James Vredenburgh, Phil's neuro-oncologist, who thought of zebras rather than horses when he heard hoofbeats. He called the shots from DUMC and communicated to the emergency staff at Duke Raleigh Hospital. It was his order for the CT arteriogram that revealed the aortic clot. Duke University Medical Center just oozes knowledge, and Phil has been the fortunate recipient of all the medical expertise a teaching hospital provides. I have loved listening to the teaching going on as Phil has been treated. We both have been cared for by gentle spirits who have our best interests in mind. The brain tumor oncology team, who seem like family to us, have been right by our sides throughout this entire ordeal.

As we wait for Phil to be discharged this morning, I want to emphasize again that Phil is the real star of this show. He has not questioned his state, and he has followed every instruction given to him. Our plan is to get him home, reunite him with his beloved couch and the other comforts of familiar surroundings, and concentrate on getting him well. He's a tough old bird and "Nurse Ratched" is again in charge! With your continued prayers, Phil will be up and at 'em again soon!

Psalms 3: 3-4 "But you, oh Lord, are a shield around me, my glory, and the one who lifts up my head. I cry aloud to the Lord, and he answers me from his holy hill."

With much love,
Shelly

There is nothing more disconcerting than having someone you love become confused and disoriented. Trying to reason with an unreasonable person is emotionally exhausting. When Phil began talking nonsense, my thoughts immediately focused on his brain tumor. Once it was determined that his confusion could be attributed to the pain medication he was receiving, I felt somewhat better, but his behavior was still difficult to witness.

For instance, he was making dinner plans with people for which he wanted me to make reservations at various restaurants. He was asking all about my nephew Drew's boat, the only problem being that Drew does not own a boat. He thought he was seeing friends of ours on different TV programs, and while watching golf on television, he thought we were at the tournament. I quickly determined that it was better to go along with what he was saying than trying to explain that he was confused. I, along with the others who came to visit, decided to just enjoy the show. We knew he was OK, so laughing became therapeutic!

In spite of all Phil had been through, he was making good progress. The medical staff assured me that Phil was doing well enough to be discharged from the hospital. As he was being prepared for discharge, I was trying to prepare myself for what I would need to do at home to make Phil comfortable and to make it easy for him to ambulate in our house. I was also trying to prepare myself mentally for being totally in charge of Phil without the luxury of having nurses and doctors right outside the door.

As uncomfortable as it was to sleep in a chair for a week, I would have slept on the floor if it meant that someone else was in charge. I was overwrought with anxiety, but I had to remain upbeat and confident as we walked out of the doors of Duke Hospital and began our trip back home. Once we arrived back at our house, Phil resumed his position on the couch and began his recovery from major surgery. As the days passed and we talked more about what he had experienced, he shared with me that he had no recollection of his hospitalization. I was floored. It must be frustrating to lose track of time, but again, maybe it's the mind's way of coping with a horrific experience.

Although Phil did not remember the actual hospitalization and surgery, his long, painful incision was a constant reminder. He took his pain medication and was determined to get better as soon as possible so that he could return to work. As crazy as it sounds, and as uncomfortable as he was, Phil seemed more like his old self than at any time since his brain surgery 10 months earlier. Being off chemotherapy made such a difference. Although he was weak and uncomfortable, it was a different weakness. As he recovered, he was able to regain some strength. The chemotherapy-induced fatigue was a different story. It never improved. I was concerned though because he had no appetite, and he wasn't sleeping that well.

July 19, 2011 6:18pm

I think we have all heard the saying "The best defense is a good offense." After Phil was seen by his oncologist at Duke today, I came home and "googled" this quote. The gist of the quote is if you can take your opponent out before your opponent starts to consider taking you out, you don't need any other defense. This seems to be the case for Phil and his brain tumor. After his tumor, his "opponent" so to speak, was diagnosed, it was completely removed by Dr. Friedman. Following his surgery, the "opponent" was bombarded by targeted radiation and then subjected to six months of intense chemotherapy. Because his team of doctors developed an offensive plan that skillfully attacked the "opponent" early in the game, it appears that Phil does not need any other defense. He will have another MRI on August 16th, and if it is clear, there will be no additional chemo, and Phil will just continue to be followed very closely by the brain tumor team.

Being followed closely means having MRIs every two months, a small price to pay for the peace of mind that it will provide. Only if there is evidence of tumor progression, will further treatment be indicated. Needless to say, Phil is no longer enrolled in a clinical trial, but lasting six months on the trial was a good milestone to reach. Studies have shown significant benefit of six months of treatment with Avastin® plus Temodar®. It is considered "standard of care." Therefore, we will move forward with the confidence that Phil has received the treatment he needed and that hopefully, he will reap the benefits of the treatment for a long, long time.

Tomorrow will mark two weeks since Phil's surgery. Although he seems to be healing well, incisional pain is causing him discomfort. He has difficulties getting into a comfortable position, and because the muscles in his back are compensating for his abdominal muscles, he is having back pain, as well. He can't sleep, and he doesn't want to eat. To sum it up, he feels pretty crummy. I remind him every morning that each day will be better, which is easy for me to say. Phil pushes through each day though with the hope of better days to come. I feel sure he is about to turn the corner on this thing, but our patience is being tested as we wait.

Shortly after Phil's surgery, I was walking the halls of Duke Hospital and had the good fortune of running into the "Angel Lady." This sweet woman works in housekeeping in the hospital, and she wears a hat covered with a variety of angel pins. I could not help but ask her about her hat. She said "Honey, it's a ministry." I must have given her a look that precipitated further explanation. She said "Honey, when you took the time to ask me about my hat covered in angel pins, it took your mind off your troubles. See, it's a ministry." I have thought of her often and of what she said to me. Each time I think of her, it does take my mind off my worries. I believe she was an angel placed in my path that day to minister to me, and I'm hoping that others stop her and ask about her special hat.

Phil has an appointment with his surgeon next Wednesday, and I'll give another update then. Until that time, please pray for Phil's physical healing and renewed strength. Thank you for being so faithful to both of us as we continue down this road to recovery.

Psalms 91:11 "He will give His angels charge of you, to guard you in all your ways."

Love,
Shelly

Just 13 days after Phil's surgery we were back in Clinic 1K for Phil's regular appointment with his brain tumor team. He was too weak and sore to walk, so Courtney met us with a wheelchair as we pulled up in front of the hospital. Phil was pitiful. I knew he was so uncomfortable, but he refused to give in to his discomfort. He was determined to show the folks in 1K that he was going to conquer this latest hurdle.

When we arrived in the clinic, he was treated like a superstar! All the nurses and doctors came to see him. Everyone who saw him told him what a lucky guy he was to have survived such a gruesome malady. I think that pleased him and gave him a little lift. His exam was uneventful, and we left knowing that we would be back on August 16th for another MRI.

22

IT'S GOING TO TAKE TIME

July 27, 2011 7:17pm

Patience: the capacity to accept or tolerate delay, trouble, or suffering without getting angry or upset.

Phil had his first post-operative visit with the vascular surgeons today, and although he received a good report, he was told that it was going to take some time before he would feel like himself again. He was reminded that he had undergone a big surgery and that 3 to 6 months would be a reasonable expectation for time to recovery. It was explained that it could take 1 to 2 months just for his body to rid itself of the anesthesia. Although frustrating, the insomnia, lack of appetite, incisional pain, weakness, and fatigue, are just part of the healing process. We were told his sleep issues could last up to 3 months and his weakness for up to 6 months. Of course, after we heard all of this, I was feeling so awful for Phil, but the next thing I heard was Phil asking when he could drive and when he could return to work! He was told 4-6 weeks post surgery before he could drive, and as far as work goes, he was told that once he feels up to it, he could go in for a couple of hours.

I have been trying to get Phil out of the house each day just to give him a change of scenery and to try and build up his endurance. He has suffered through many a mundane errand, but I try to convince him that it is making him stronger! He did manage to take a giant step toward recovery when he made a trip to Costco! He walked inside long enough to pick out 3 new pairs of shorts that he'll be able to wear until he gets back to his "playing" weight.

The best news we received today was hearing that Phil has been cleared to go back to the beach! Aynsley will be arriving Friday evening with Mary Weldon, Greer, Martha, and Harris, and on Saturday, we will all head east! We're hoping that Mary Chandler and Louisa will be able to join us, as well. As Phil said, he can lie on the couch in Emerald Isle as well as he can lie on the couch in Raleigh. Being surrounded by children and grandchildren will be the best medicine of all!

The past three weeks have been challenging ones at best. It's funny; Phil has very little recall of his hospital experience, which is a good thing I guess. Both of us were getting discouraged with what seemed to be a lack of recuperative progress; however, after hearing what we did today, our feeling of relief was almost palpable. Just hearing that everything Phil is experiencing is completely expected did wonders for us. Reassurance is a powerful thing! We will now move forward with more realistic expectations knowing that, with time, Phil will recover from his surgery. All of this redefines patience.

As I come to the end of another post, I must again thank each of you who follow Phil's progress and so faithfully support us. As I have said before, there are so many of you I have never met, but this fact in no way diminishes my feelings of gratitude. We are a blessed family, and we continue to reap the rewards of devoted friends and family. You know who you are.

2 Corinthians 12:10 "Therefore I am content with weaknesses, insults, hardships, persecutions, and calamities for the sake of Christ; for whenever I am weak, then I am strong."

Love,
Shelly

For 7 weeks, all I could think about was helping Phil recover from major abdominal surgery. I tried everything I could to help him regain his strength. His appetite was nonexistent and as a result, he experienced significant weight loss and fatigue. I finally found something he seemed to "enjoy"...a peanut butter smoothie.

I would go to the neighborhood smoothie store and have them add every booster possible to get Phil's peanut butter smoothie close to 1000 calories. The rest of the calories were left up to me. I was cooking everything imaginable in hopes of hitting on something that would appeal to Phil. I would present him with what I thought would be very appetizing snacks and meals only to have him refuse to eat. To someone like me who thought I was personally responsible for getting Phil well, it was totally frustrating. I could not understand how he could not make himself eat, especially when I was going out of my way to prepare good food. When he did not eat, I felt like a failure. I was becoming more and more anxious, fearful that he was going to start failing.

I knew he needed to feed his body not only to promote healing but also to regain his strength and stamina. I was being held captive by the entire situation. I wasn't nearly as concerned about Phil's brain tumor as I was about his physical condition and getting him back to what I considered "normal." He was in a vicious cycle...too fatigued to eat which fueled further fatigue. He was supposed to be walking every day, but it exhausted him to walk to the bathroom.

My response was to try to be upbeat. I would tell Phil how well he was doing in hopes that it would empower him to believe he was doing better. In retrospect, Phil was getting better physically, but not as quickly as I had hoped. I just wanted my husband back.

When Phil had his first post-operative visit, we had many of our concerns assuaged. I had made a list of questions, and as I posed each one, we were reassured that everything we were concerned about was completely normal and expected. While my questions centered around Phil's physical condition and when we could expect significant improvement, all Phil wanted to know was when he could drive and return to work. It was like an "aha" moment for me, because it suddenly became very clear that while I was hung up on his physical condition, Phil defined healing and doing better by his ability to return to work.

August 16, 2011 9:27pm

Time goes by so quickly, and before you know it, two months have passed, and it's time for Phil to have another MRI. Today was that day. Since his last dose of Avastin® was on June 24th, we were anxious to see if that would have any effect on the MRI results. When we saw Dr. Vredenburgh, it was explained to us that Phil's MRI did look different compared to his previous MRI on June 21st; however, Dr. "V" was confident that the changes he saw are attributable to the absence of Avastin® and not to reoccurrence of the tumor. There was no evidence of any increased swelling, which is a good thing, and Phil's neurological exam was totally normal.

To be on the safe side, Dr. V wants to repeat the MRI in a month. If his assumption is correct, Phil will continue on his course of having repeat MRIs every 2 months. If the MRI shows a regrowth of the tumor, Phil will begin taking Temodar®, the oral chemotherapy, five days out of a 28-day cycle. We're not going to think about recurrent tumors and/or chemotherapy until we have to. September 13th will be a very important date, as that Tuesday is the day we'll have many questions answered.

Dr. Vredenburgh and his staff marveled at the progress Phil has made since his last visit, which was just 13 days after his surgery. His blood counts are normal, and his weight has remained stable. They called Phil a very, very lucky man to have survived the aortic blood clot and subsequent surgery. I'm convinced he has an army of angels surrounding him!

Last week marked the real beginning of Phil's comeback when he returned to work for a couple of hours for a few days. He is building up his stamina in hopes of returning to work full-time, sooner than later.

As we drove to the beach last weekend, Garth Brooks's song "I will Sail My Vessel" came on the radio, and I could not help but feel that the lyrics describe Phil's journey this past year. Believe it or not, September 1st marks the year anniversary of Phil's diagnosis. It has been a year of highs and lows, but I think the highs have won. We have learned to "let go and let God." We have been sustained by the love of family and friends. Through adversity, we have made new friends with whom we share a common bond. We have learned the meaning of trust - trusting the incredibly skilled physicians to guide us and care for Phil, always having his best interest in mind. It has also been a year of renewed faith. We know that God has a plan for Phil and for those who love him. Again, a lesson in trust.

As we wait another 4 weeks for confirmation of the meaning of the MRI changes, I would ask that you pray for peace of mind for Phil. Please pray too that he will continue to improve and regain his strength. I have to remind myself that the doctors said it could take 6 months before he recovers completely from the surgery. It all boils down to trust.

Hebrews 2:13 "And again, I will put my trust in him."

Love,
Shelly

I Will Sail My Vessel

You know a dream is like a river,
Ever changing as it flows,
and the dreamer is just a vessel,
that must follow where it goes.

Trying to learn from what's behind you,
and never knowing what's in store.
Makes each day a constant battle,
just to stay between the shores.

And I will sail my vessel,
till the river runs dry.
Like a bird upon the wind,
these waters are my sky.
I'll never reach my destination
If I never try,
So I will sail my vessel,
till the river runs dry!

Too many times we stand aside,
and let the water slip away.
And what we put off till tomorrow,
has now become today.
So don't you sit upon the shore line,
and say you're satisfied.
Choose the chance to rapids,
and dare to dance the tides.

Chorus

There is bound to be rough waters,
and I know I'll take some falls,
with the good lord as my captain,
I can make it through them all!

As always, when it came to treating Phil's brain tumor, we placed all our trust in Dr. V, as we should have; he was an expert and we accepted whatever he told us to be true. When he told us that he was confident the changes he saw on Phil's MRI were a result of the discontinuation of the Avastin®, there was no reason for us to question his medical expertise. What we were to learn later is that it's difficult to discern whether MRI changes indicate tumor progression, radiation necrosis, or in Phil's case, the recent cessation of Avastin®. To be 100% sure of what MRI changes represent, one must have a PET scan where the findings will be conclusive.

In Phil's case, Dr. V made the decision to repeat Phil's MRI in a month, and then if the changes were still there, we would proceed with a PET scan. Unbeknownst to us, Dr. V's decision gave us another month to enjoy living our lives thinking that Phil's condition was stable.

Life seemed to be getting back to "normal" as Phil returned to work for a few hours a day. It certainly raised his spirits. Phil's job was his life. He truly lived to work, and he loved being with his co-workers.

23

A NOTE FROM PHIL

September 7, 2011 5:41pm

It has been a number of months since I have contributed to the updates that Shelly has been so proficient in doing. I'll try to keep it brief.

I am becoming fearful of the sixth day of the month. One year ago, my brain surgery was done on September 6, 2010. Two months ago, on July 6, 2011, I had major surgery to clean out a blockage in my aorta that was about 8" long creating a blockage of 85% of the blood flow. My doctors attribute the blockage to the medicines I was on and not to good food like pork skins! Next Tuesday, the 13th, I will have another MRI to hopefully verify that my tumor is not growing back. It will be a nerve-racking day I am sure, so if you have a moment, say a little prayer for the results and my attitude.

The past 12 months have flown by. Overall, my attitude has been that, with the help of the Lord, I am going to win this challenge. It has been trying from time to time, but slowly I am regaining my strength. I have been working part-time since August 8th, just 4 weeks after my last surgery. I'm hoping to make it a full day soon. My staff has backed me up, and I'm afraid they'll soon recognize that they don't need me!

I never look at my Caring Bridge site without being amazed at the kind thoughts and words of support being expressed by so many of you. It has also become painfully clear that many of you go to my site just to read Shelly's updates, rather than to see how I am doing. I don't blame you as I have enjoyed her updates, as well. Isn't she wonderful?

God bless each of you, and especially Shelly, Aynsley, and Mary Chandler. They take good care of me! I'm still one of the lucky ones.

Phil

24

WORRISOME CHANGES

September 13, 2011 6:26pm

I'm giving you all a very condensed update because we still don't know a lot. Phil had his scheduled MRI today, and it showed further changes consistent with either tumor progression or radiation damage resulting in what is called "pseudotumor progression." In order to determine exactly what is going on, Phil will have a "PET" scan tomorrow morning at 9:45. Unfortunately, it will take another 24 hours before the results will be available. Therefore, it will be sometime on Thursday before we have the answers we were so in hopes of receiving today.

Phil has been doing so well with no symptoms of tumor recurrence. His last two neuro exams have been totally normal. We are cautiously optimistic and will hope and pray for good results from the PET scan. As soon as we hear from Dr. V on Thursday, I will update Phil's site with the latest information. Until that time, please continue to pray.

Isaiah 12:2 "Surely God is my salvation; I will trust, and will not be afraid, for the Lord God is my strength and my might; he has become my salvation."

Love,
Shelly

Just when I thought our lives were getting back on track and beginning to resemble what I would describe as normal, we were rocked with the news that Phil's MRI showed changes... tumor progression or pseudotumor progression, the doctors weren't sure. It would take a PET scan to confirm the diagnosis. Because Phil seemed to be doing so well, returning to work for a few hours a day and just seeming to be more like himself, I wasn't worried about the PET scan. I was confident it would show pseudotumor progression and that we would just get on with the task of keeping his tumor at bay via whatever means the doctors prescribed.

September 14, 2011 3:13pm

"The race is not to the swift, but to those who keep on running."

As planned, Phil went back to Duke today for his scheduled PET scan. We have just heard back from the oncologist who informed us that the PET scan was "hot," meaning that the tumor has in fact recurred. Although it's not the news we wanted to hear, the oncology team was very encouraging. Phil will go back on a low dose of chemotherapy (Temodar®) that he will take on a daily basis. Added to his regimen will be Etoposide, another chemotherapeutic agent he will take for 12 days and be off of for 16 days. Phil's oncology team will put their collective heads together to determine if Phil is a candidate for "gamma knife radiation," which is a procedure that radiates just the specific tumor site. If he does have this radiation, it will either be a one-day treatment or a treatment in which Phil will go for 5 days in a row. We will just wait to hear what the decision is. In the meantime, we will follow the instructions given to us and go about our lives as we have been.

With the type of brain tumor Phil has, we always knew that it would come back some day; we were hoping that it would not be quite this soon. With that being said, we do not feel defeated at all. Quite the contrary.

We were in Montgomery, Al last weekend for the baptism of our grandson, Harris. The sermon on Sunday was based on Ephesians 6:10-20 where it speaks about putting on the whole armor of God. We were reminded that wearing this armor prepares us for whatever challenges come our way. How timely for us to hear those words. Phil and I are putting on the "whole armor of God" and we are fighting Phil's foe head on! Thanks be to God.

Love,
Shelly

As I drove around Raleigh running errands, I received a call from Phil's nurse practitioner. She asked that I pull over or park so that we could talk. With this request, intuitively I knew I would not be hearing good news.

She went on to explain that Phil's PET scan was "hot," confirmation that the tumor was back. I was not surprised, but I was disappointed to hear the news. I asked Christina what the results meant in terms of disease progression and outcome. I point blank asked her how long people usually lived after recurrence of a GBM. She paused and then said "The data say 6 months." She also said that she had a patient with recurrent disease who comes in about every 6 months, has his tumor radiated and then goes on about his business until he needs to come back again for further treatment.

For some reason, I believed that this could be Phil's story too. However, it was not to be.

October 2, 2011 8:07pm

Phil is hanging tough!

Tuesday, September 20th, marked the start of Phil's new chemotherapy regimen. He is taking Temodar® on a daily basis and Etoposide for 12 days out of a 28-day cycle. Since Phil had taken the same dose of Temodar® a year ago without any problems, we felt confident that it would again be well-tolerated. The new kid on the block, Etoposide, would prove to be a different story. After suffering significant nausea last weekend, Phil had to try a different approach with dosing his Zofran® (anti-nausea medication). Now that he is taking it every 8 hours around the clock, he is feeling fine. October 17th will be the date of his next MRI. On October 18th, we will meet with Dr. Vredenburgh who will inform us of the MRI results, which will be indicative of how well the new chemo regimen is working. Following that appointment, we will meet with Phil's radiation oncologist who will evaluate him for the Gamma Knife radiation and schedule the date(s) for his treatment.

It has been almost 3 months since Phil's surgery, and I am really seeing a difference in how he feels. His appetite continues to improve and his energy level is picking up. He is showing renewed interest in activities he enjoys. When we were at the beach last weekend, he played golf. Unfortunately, the golf outing was cut short by torrential rain, and from what Phil described, the weather mercifully put an end to a horrendous personal performance on his part. Oh well, maybe a trip to the driving range is in order! He is working in his shop and enjoying a good cigar!! The Credit Union is his mainstay in life, and he loves going to work!!

When Phil was first diagnosed with his brain tumor, I described it as jumping into a "black hole." A black hole is defined as a region of space having a gravitational field so intense that no matter or radiation can escape. Although I still feel this way, I realize that we are tethered in that black hole by you, our family and friends, and the countless number of prayers being said on our behalf. It is our belief that the gravitational field of those prayers is stronger than the gravitational field of any disease. Thank you for continuing to pray for Phil. He is filled with hope, and never do I hear a complaint. Borrowing from a sermon, and I am paraphrasing...hope gives us the courage to face the unknown. Amen.

Daniel 10:19 "He said, Do not fear, greatly beloved, you are safe. Be strong and courageous! When he spoke to me, I was strengthened and said, Let my lord speak, for you have strengthened me."

Love,

Shelly

October 7, 2011 was the wedding date of the son of very dear friends of ours. The wedding was in Morehead City, NC (a 25 minute drive from Emerald Isle) so Phil and I decided we would go. Phil was feeling well and looking forward to the weekend, which translated into excitement for me. We were planning a great weekend in Emerald Isle where we would attend a wedding, walk on the beach, and just enjoy being together. We left mid-morning on Friday, and as soon as we reached our cottage, Phil expressed a desire to go for a walk on the beach. He wanted to take the dogs, so I offered to drive him and the dogs to the beach access where I would drop them off, drive back to our house, and then walk to meet them.

There are benches at the public access so Phil could rest as he waited for me to get back. Once I made the short walk back to the beach access, we began our stroll on the beach. We had walked about 10 minutes when Phil told me he was ready to return home. I was walking a little bit in front of him, and when I heard him say he wanted to head back to the beach house, I realized his legs must be giving out. I turned around to him and told him to sit down on the beach. It was as though he could not process what I was saying to him. He had our dog Tapper on the leash, and he wouldn't let go. He kept turning in circles, which wrapped the leash around his legs. I began screaming at him to let go of the leash and to sit down! He would not let go. After turning in circles for what seemed like an eternity, he fell. I couldn't break his fall.

What I hadn't noticed during this time was the beach patrol who had been riding down the beach; they had witnessed the entire episode. Phil had no sooner hit the ground that they were right there! They immediately radioed for help. I pleaded with them not to call an ambulance. I explained that he had a brain tumor and that his fall was related to his weakened condition. Phil was not the least bit concerned and politely asked them if they would give him a ride back to our cottage. After much discussion, they agreed to do so. I took the leashes of both dogs and walked back home.

As I turned onto our driveway, I saw Phil sitting on the bench outside our door. It was all I could do to make that walk home. My mind raced. I felt sick. What did this mean? What started out as a weekend I was so excited about, was quickly turning into the reality I was trying to escape. As I had driven to the beach, I was thinking about what fun we were going to have. Phil seemed to be doing so well. I was dreaming of dancing with him at the wedding, going out to eat, and walking on the beach. All of these plans came crashing down within an hour of arriving in Emerald Isle.

The next morning Phil accepted an invitation to play golf with 2 friends from Raleigh. After the events of the previous afternoon, I was excited that he wanted to play. The weather was threatening, but the threesome set out to play 18 holes. They only made it through 9 holes before heavy rain forced them to stop play. When

Phil returned home, he shared with me that he had thrown up on the second hole. It made me so sad to hear that. He was trying so hard to keep going as though everything was OK.

That afternoon we dressed for the wedding and drove to Morehead City for the event. After Phil's fall on the beach, I was terrified that it would happen again. I held his arm as though I would be able to keep him from falling. As silly as that was, it gave me peace of mind.

The wedding was beautiful, we saw lots of friends from Raleigh and Greenville, NC, the bride's hometown, and we looked forward to visiting more at the reception. As we drove to the reception site, it became apparent that Phil was getting more fatigued. Before he had to ask that the evening be cut short, I suggested that we go in, say hello to the bride and groom, have something to eat, and then return home. He agreed to the plan. We were at the reception for about an hour where we remained seated the entire time. There were the cursory hellos from people, but my dream of dancing, mingling among the crowd, and celebrating with the bride and groom were not realized.

I was so sad for Phil and for us as a couple. In my heart I knew what this meant: I had once again set my expectations too high; Phil and I would never dance again.

October 18, 2011 7:18pm

As the saying goes, "When the going gets tough, the tough get going." That is now our new mantra. As much as I would like to report good news, I'm afraid the news is not good.

Phil had another MRI late yesterday afternoon, and we were back at Duke bright and early this morning to see both the radiation oncologist and the neuro-oncologist. One doctor said the tumor had doubled in size since the last MRI, and another said it had quadrupled in size. Regardless of who is more accurate in their assessment, the bottom line is the tumor has gotten significantly larger than it was a month ago. The chemotherapy regimen seemed to act as fertilizer rather than killing the tumor cells as we had all hoped it would do.

So, it's time again to drop back and punt and start with a new playbook. Here is the plan: Starting next Monday, Phil will receive 5 straight days of "Gamma Knife radiation." He will receive 500 units of radiation/treatment (compared to the 180 units of radiation/treatment last year) to the targeted area. Rather than the wide burst of radiation he received previously, this radiation field will have very tight margins, focusing solely on the recurrent tumor. After the radiation treatment is completed, Phil will have a week off before a new chemotherapeutic regimen is begun.

Again, the chemo will be administered orally. He'll be on CCNU (1 capsule every 6 weeks) and Rapamycin®, (dosed 3 times a week) two drugs that have been around for a while. The doctors will also be bringing back an old friend/foe, Avastin®. Because of the efficacy of the combination treatment of Avastin® and radiation, Phil's doctors feel that the benefits of administering the drug outweigh the risks of developing another arterial clot. To maximize the effects of the Avastin®, he will receive a 6-month course of the drug. Phil's next MRI, scheduled for December 20th, will reveal the effectiveness of this protocol. It's a waiting game. Although we have become accustomed to "waiting" for the next MRI results, it doesn't get any easier. With that being said, we continue to make "living in the moment" our goal.

Thank you for your continued prayers and good wishes. We feel them and treasure them. I will continue to update this site when it is warranted. Please interpret no news to mean good news, or no change in Phil's status. I would ask that you specifically pray that Phil responds favorably to the Gamma Knife radiation and to the new chemo protocol.

Psalm 121: "I lift my eyes to the hills-from where will my help come? My help comes from the Lord, who made heaven and earth."

With love and a grateful heart,
Shelly

October 17th is my birthday, and it just so happened that Phil was scheduled for an MRI late that afternoon. The plan was for him to have his MRI, after which we would drive to Streets of Southpoint Mall in Durham to meet Mary Chandler, Scott, and Louisa for an early supper to celebrate my birthday. Everything went as planned, and the 5 of us had supper at Firebirds Rocky Mountain Grill. Because the weather was so nice, we decided to eat outside. However, as we were eating, Phil announced that he was finished and that he was going to go to the Apple Store and buy an iPhone.

I was furious! I pleaded with him to stay until the rest of us had finished our meals, but nothing I said could convince him to wait. At this point, I was having trouble separating the disease from the man. It was my birthday, and all I wanted was to have a nice meal with my family. Here Phil was wandering off again, and I didn't know what was going to happen. It was very reminiscent of the experience we had in Florida when all he could think about was the new Droid phone he wanted, and I was not happy.

Mary Chandler, Scott and I caught up with Phil in the Apple Store, and after they said good-bye to him, they drove back to Greensboro. I, on the other hand, spent the next 4 hours with Phil in the Apple store as he negotiated the purchase of his new phone. I ran back and forth between the Verizon store and the Apple store trying to cancel out one contract while he was setting up another. I was exhausted and frustrated. I wanted nothing more than to just go home. At 10:00 that night, we finally left the Apple store.

Once we got to the car and were pulling out of the parking lot, Phil experienced his first episode of bladder incontinence. It didn't bother him at all. He simply announced it to me and pro-ceeded to play with his new phone. I was heartsick. It was further confirmation that the next day would be a pivotal one. I knew the doctors were not going to have good news for us. I was correct.

When we were informed that the tumor had in fact returned, Dr. V recommended that Phil undergo Gamma Knife Radiation. We again found ourselves consulting with Dr. Kirkpatrick about his plan of action for Phil's treatment. I questioned the success rate of the procedure never expecting the answer I received. Dr. Kirkpatrick quickly blurted out "Most people will live a year after treatment." My reaction was visceral. I thought I was going to be physically ill. I could hardly breathe. Phil sat motionless and quiet. I don't know what I thought we would be told, but I wasn't prepared for what I had heard. For some reason, I thought this Gamma Knife Radiation was going to be the ticket. It would blast the tumor once and for all. How naive I was! We left the exam room and returned to our car. As we were driving home, I asked Phil what he thought about all that he had heard during our time at Duke that day. He said "Well, I didn't like what Dr. Kirkpatrick said." I didn't know what to say, so in typical cheerleader style, I said "Well, we're just not going to think that way." We drove in silence the rest of the way home.

25

Much Needed
Time Away

November 8, 2011 7:59am

Not sure who is having more fun!

Friends and family, I am writing to you from Montgomery, Alabama where I have been since last Saturday when Phil left for New Orleans. As I said in the title, I don't know who is having more fun, Phil or me? I'll let you be the judge.

Phil got the go ahead from his doctors at Duke to attend a conference in New Orleans where he was to speak on "Decentralized Lending." He has done great! He made it through 2 presentations and from what he has described, the food he has consumed would rival any on the cover of Gourmet Magazine! Not only has he had the opportunity to catch up with old friends at the conference, but also to have Sunday brunch with my step-brother Grady, who lives in New Orleans. Going to this conference has been a real boost for Phil, and I am so happy he has been feeling well enough to enjoy it.

When Phil left for the airport in the wee hours of the morning last Saturday, I left for Greensboro, where I picked up Mary Chandler and

Louisa to begin our trip to the deep south. It's never too early to introduce the concept of a "girls' trip" to a baby girl. Since arriving in Montgomery, I have seen Martha's preschool class, accompanied her to ballet class, and watched several dramatic performances choreographed by her older sister Mary Weldon and directed by her older brother Greer. I have had the opportunity to listen to a Thanksgiving report from Mary Weldon where she described in great detail the very first Thanksgiving. Last night, I attended Greer's first indoor soccer game and had the privilege of listening to him read 2 books to me. Harris and Louisa, (8 months) who are a week apart in age, have provided non-stop entertainment as they discover the joys of playing with one another.

I guess what I am trying to say is that Phil and I both needed a break from the realities of life. He found his break among dear work friends, and I found mine surrounded by children and grandchildren. We both head home tomorrow, equipped to get back in the ring to keep on fighting.

Just to bring you up to date, Phil received 5 days of stereotactic radiosurgery, which is just high-dose radiation to the tumor site (I had mistakenly been calling it "gamma knife radiation."). He completed his treatment on Friday, October 28th. The doctors agreed to wait until Phil returned from New Orleans before starting his new chemo routine. On November 11th, he will add 2 new drugs to his treatment regimen in hopes of keeping his tumor in check. We will not know how effective the radiation and chemo have been until December 20th when he has another MRI.

In the meantime, I am trying to keep in mind a quote from Archibald D. Hart: "Worry involves relying on self rather than on God, and it gets in the way of faith."

Love,
Shelly

When I left Raleigh on my way to Greensboro to pick up Mary Chandler and Louisa, I was filled with a multitude of emotions. I was excited, relieved, filled with a sense of freedom, yet also feeling somewhat guilty about how much I was looking forward to going on this trip with JUST Mary Chandler and Louisa. The anticipation of being relieved of my responsibilities as caretaker for several days gave me a sense of euphoria. I couldn't wait to spend time with our girls and our grandchildren when I could devote 100% of myself to just them. I was also aware that Montgomery is only 4 hours from New Orleans so if Phil needed me, I could get there quickly. That fact did offer me comfort and made me feel better about our respective trips. Both Phil and I enjoyed ourselves, and I was so glad that we had moved forward with our plans. It would have been easier and emotionally safer to just say no and stay home.

For my birthday, Aynsley and Mary Chandler surprised me by giving me a weekend trip to Asheville, North Carolina that also included a tour of the Biltmore House. The plan was for Aynsley and her family to drive up from Montgomery the weekend before Thanksgiving and meet Phil, Mary Chandler, Scott, Louisa and me at a home the girls had rented in Black Mountain. By 8:00 that night, we were all together exploring the beautiful home that would be ours for the weekend and planning our time at Biltmore and in downtown Asheville. Phil and I stayed on the main floor so that he did not have to navigate any stairs. Although he tired easily, he was acting more like himself and enjoying the grandchildren and all of the activity surrounding him. The plan was for Aynsley, Mary Chandler, Mary Weldon, Greer, and me to tour the Biltmore House and then meet the boys and the other 3 children in downtown Asheville for lunch. The first part of our plan worked flawlessly. The tour of the Biltmore House surpassed all expectations! It was decorated for Christmas, which to me, elevated the overall beauty of such a national treasure. There was so much history surrounding the home and its owners; it was almost too much to take in during one visit. After our tour, we left the grounds heading to downtown Asheville to meet the rest of the family for lunch.

What we hadn't planned on was finding ourselves in the middle of the Asheville Christmas parade! Meeting up with the rest of our group was a challenge and finding a place to eat, a bigger challenge. Once we did reunite with Phil, Cade, Scott and the 3 little ones, we had to walk several blocks to find a restaurant that could accommodate 6 adults and five children. Watching Phil grow more and more weary was really troublesome for me. I was so worried about him falling. We didn't try to keep up with the others. We made sure to keep them in sight as they looked for somewhere to eat. The fabulous restaurants friends had recommended had to be set aside for another trip; the wait times were simply too long. We had to settle for pizza, but no one complained. It was good to get inside and sit down as I could tell Phil was struggling. The rest of the weekend was uneventful, and on Sunday, we all returned to Raleigh.

The changes in Phil's physical condition were subtle; however, I could tell that the weekend in Asheville had taken its toll. As it always is, Thanksgiving Day was spent at my brother's house. We were all together and were able to enjoy an unseasonably warm day. Phil was very quiet and spent most of his time sitting in a recliner in the den with different family members addressing any need he had. Although I didn't say anything to anyone, I was concerned. Things were different. In less than 2 weeks, Phil would be back in the hospital.

26

AN UNEXPECTED TURN

December 6, 2011 4:41am

Days start early in the hospital...a 4:00 am blood pressure check and orientation status (how can anyone be oriented to place and time at 4:00 am?), a 5:00 am visit from the lab to draw blood, and the endless sounds of monitors and chatter among hospital staff. Yes, that's what Phil is waking up to today. But let me backtrack.

Phil was seen by his neuro-oncology team last Tuesday and had a totally normal exam. He received his Avastin® treatment as planned and returned home. He went to work on Wednesday and Thursday but became increasingly fatigued. He gave in to his fatigue on Friday and slept at least 20 hrs out of a 24-hr period. However, chemotherapy-induced fatigue is like an unquenchable thirst; it is not totally relieved by rest. In addition to his fatigue, his legs became very weak and he began to suffer from slight confusion.

When Monday morning came, I reported all of this to his team of healthcare professionals. They advised that his MRI, originally scheduled for December 20th, be moved to Monday. As we were preparing to leave for his appointment, Phil fell in the bathroom, hitting his head on the tub, and putting a large gash over his left eye. Instead of heading to Lennox Baker for an MRI, we were on our way to the Duke ER for a CT scan to rule out an intracranial bleed and for Phil's cut to be sutured. I assured him we would make up a much better story to explain his injury...like how he got into a fight defending my honor...sounds better than cracking one's head open on a bath tub! Anyway, it was decided that it would be in Phil's best interest to be admitted for observation. He eventually had his MRI last night at 10:30!

We will meet with his oncologist today to hear the results and discuss next steps. In the meantime, Phil continues to be a shining example of bravery, resilience, and hope. As we await the results of his most recent tests, I am reminded of a quote from Corrie Ten Boom: "Never be afraid to trust an unknown future to a known God." Thank you for your continued prayers.

Love,
Shelly

Mary Chandler knew Phil was struggling with both confusion and fatigue, so she volunteered to come to Raleigh and go with us to his MRI appointment. I welcomed her presence. While she took Louisa to her other grandmother's house, I helped Phil get dressed and ready to go. He was really slow that morning and just when I thought he had his coat on and was ready to leave, he announced that he needed to use the bathroom. I wanted so badly to say "no, just go when we get to Lennox Baker." We needed to leave soon, and Phil was notorious for his long stays in the bathroom. He wasn't in the bathroom long before I heard a terrible thud; I knew immediately that he had fallen.

I screamed and ran toward the bathroom, which has two entrances, one in the foyer hallway and the other in the downstairs bedroom. When I tried to open the door in the hall, I realized that Phil was lodged up against it. I ran around through the bedroom to the other entrance and found Phil head down in the bathtub and blood everywhere! As I pulled his upper body out of the tub, I tried to determine the source of his bleeding. I finally realized he had a significant cut in his eyebrow over his left eye. Mary Chandler walked in the house about this time, and I yelled to her to bring a wet towel and some ice. I cleaned Phil's face and made an icepack for him to use until we could make it to the hospital. I asked Mary Chandler to drive, and I sat in the backseat with Phil. I immediately called our brain tumor team at Duke and alerted them as to what was going on. In light of his fall and subsequent cut, they advised me to take him straight to the emergency room.

Phil was pitiful. He didn't say a word, but when the ER staff began asking him questions and he started answering, it was obvious he was very confused. Due to confusion and decreased mentation, he was admitted for further testing. Other than the cut over his left eye, I didn't have a clue as to what was going on and what I should expect. I was scared.

December 6, 2011 10:36am

Y'all aren't going to believe this!!!

I am writing to share some fabulous news with you! Dr. Desjardin just came in with the results of Phil's latest MRI, and it is totally clear!!! She said she had to look at it several times to make sure she was looking at the right MRI! I've decided we may have to use the pictures as this year's Christmas card! At least we wouldn't have to argue about what everyone was wearing!!

Anyway, these results are miraculous in that Dr. V told us the best we could hope for would be to have the recurrent tumor remain stable. We are so relieved to say the least. Now, on to what they think is going on with Phil...pneumonia! I never thought I would be happy to report that Phil has a probable pneumonia. He is having a CT scan this afternoon to verify the diagnosis and also to verify the location (which lobe) of the pneumonia. The doctors think it is PCP (pneumocystis pneumonia), a pneumonia seen in people with compromised immune systems. Depending on the lobe(s) that is affected, Phil will have either IV and oral antibiotics, or just oral antibiotics. Either way, he will be here at least another day. Many thanks to you, our dear family and friends, for your continued prayers and support. Our love for you is immeasurable.

Shelly

When one is fatigued, mentally exhausted and hoping against hope, it's easy to hear news and interpret it to mean something that it's not. That's exactly what happened when we received the news that Phil's MRI was clear. I immediately thought the stereotactic radiation had been successful in destroying the tumor that had returned in Phil's head. Although his clinical picture did not agree with the results we were hearing, it didn't matter to me. His MRI was clear and that's what was important. I was to find out later that MRIs performed within a short period of time following stereotactic surgery can give, for lack of a better explanation, false negative results. Although a tumor can still be present, the intense radiation given during the treatment "clouds" the picture.

Phil also had a CT scan that ruled out pneumonia, pulmonary emboli, and RSV, but it did reveal a small clot in one of his sinuses. In hopes of preventing the formation of further clots, Phil began receiving Lovenox®, a low weight heparin, that he would need to take for 6 months. Although I was relieved that Phil did not have any of the problems the medical staff thought he had at the time of admission to the hospital, I was still at a loss as to why he was so confused and sick. It seemed that people were grasping at straws.

In one of my lower moments, I was standing in the hallway down from Phil's room talking with one of Mary Chandler's friends who is a nurse at Duke. As I was talking, I caught sight of Sprague, another one of the Physician Assistants on the brain tumor team. In addition to being a high school friend of my brother's, he is also a cousin to friends of ours. Phil and I both loved our connection to him and always looked forward to seeing him when we came to Clinic 1K.

When my eyes met Sprague's I did something very uncharacteristic of me, I burst into tears. He hugged me and asked what was wrong. I told him I felt like Phil was being used as a guinea pig, and that I didn't want my husband being treated like just another number in a clinical trial. Sprague was very reassuring and calmed my fears.

I was overwrought with anxiety. The uncertainty of the entire situation had gotten the best of me. I was sleep deprived and sick of being at Duke. Phil was so confused he was driving me crazy. My patience was wearing thin. Phil kept asking to go home, and each time I told him he had to stay a little longer, he threatened to call Courtney and demand that she come up to his room and get him discharged. It was funny for a while, but after repeating this scenario over and over again, I grew weary.

By this time, Aynsley had arrived from Montgomery. Mary Chandler and I both were happy to have a new set of hands and a clear mind to help us deal with the situation at hand. Since she had not been in the middle of all that had gone on in the previous 36 hours, Aynsley could survey the state of affairs and offer objective advice. Whenever I needed a break, she would relieve me. I would drive back to Raleigh, shower, change clothes and immediately return to Duke. I would never be away for more than 2 hours. In the midst of all this madness, it was imperative that we keep our sense of humor.

One time when I had left to go home to get refreshed, I had no sooner pulled out of the parking deck when I received a text from Aynsley warning me that Phil would be calling me soon. In his hospital room, we had to ensure that his phone and iPad were with him at all times, or he would become frantic looking for them. Sure enough, shortly after I received the heads up from Aynsley, my phone began ringing. As expected, it was Phil. He said "Where the hell are you?" I explained that I was on my way home to get freshened up and that I would return shortly. He responded "Get in the damn car and get the hell back over here now!" I had to laugh. This was not Phil talking. He would never talk to me like this; it was his illness talking.

Phil had also developed an obsession with toothpicks! He insisted upon having a collection of toothpicks with him at all times. He had toothpicks everywhere...in every pocket, in every drawer, in his bed...you name it, a toothpick was there. Thank goodness Aynsley was there to see and hear all of this. We laughed and laughed because it was so very unlike Phil. Our laughter became a defense mechanism; it was the only way we were able to cope with Phil's bizarre behavior and our doubts about what was really going on. All I wanted were answers to questions that had no answers.

December 11, 2011 5:40pm

How wonderful it is to be back home among the people, pets, and things that bring us comfort! I feel like I am shaking an Etch-A-Sketch to erase what I have told you earlier. With the exception of the MRI results (clear in that the chemo and radiation have shrunk the tumor), all that I reported to you has changed. Please note that Phil does NOT have any of the following:

1. Pneumonia
2. RSV
3. Mini seizures
4. Pulmonary emboli

When the Brain Tumor team came to discharge Phil on Thursday, they explained to me that he did not have any of the maladies listed above. They feel that the extreme fatigue and weakness in his legs was caused by a "perfect storm" so to speak. The cumulative effects of chemo and radiation paired with a very bad chest cold and extreme exhaustion from simply trying to do too much, took its toll.

Phil has instructions from his doctors not to work for a while and to concentrate on getting as much rest as possible. They also informed us that tests had revealed a non-occlusive clot in his sigmoid sinus. Therefore, he has been placed on a blood thinner, Lovenox®, that he will take for the next

6 months. In hopes of strengthening his legs, he will also receive outpatient physical therapy, which begins on Tuesday.

We have basically moved downstairs in hopes of minimizing potential fall risks. I know I am driving Phil crazy because I follow him everywhere he goes. I would be lying if I didn't say I was worried about him falling again. If he were to fall again and hit his head, it could be catastrophic because of his being on Lovenox®. I also know he is getting bored sitting around the house "resting." I'm trying to think up fun things one can do to alleviate boredom that will not be exhausting. The best idea I have come up with is riding around looking at Christmas decorations and then swinging by Krispy Kreme to see if the hot sign is on. Of course we can't do that every night, so I'll keep thinking, and maybe I will come up with something more exciting to do AND less fattening!

We were fortunate to have both Aynsley and Mary Chandler with us last week. It was such a scary time and having them by my side gave me the peace and confidence to get through this latest crisis. Aynsley flew back on Friday, and Mary Chandler left today. Although it's just Phil and me now, as long as we have our faith, we will never be alone.

Thank you for your continued love and support.

Matthew 17:20 "For truly I tell you, if you have faith the size of a mustard seed, you will say to this mountain, move from here to there, and it will move; and nothing will be impossible for you."

Love,
Shelly

I always said I would never have an artificial Christmas tree, but I was having to give in. I knew there was no way I could go and get a live tree the size we normally buy, so I had to do the next best thing...buy one that came in 3 pieces and was already decorated with lights. I was determined to decorate our house for Christmas and make the holiday as joyful as possible as I knew in my heart this was going to be Phil's last Christmas on this earth. He lay on the couch while I decorated the tree and seemed to enjoy watching.

As always, Phil's credit union colleagues continued to be a presence in our family. They wanted to show their support for Phil and to give him a special holiday treat by coming to our house and singing Christmas Carols. I kept it a secret from him because I thought it would be a wonderful surprise to have his dear friends show up at our house with such a special gift. As I waited for their arrival, I made hot cider and cookies to offer to our carolers. Right on schedule, they arrived. Phil and I sat on the bench on our side porch as the group of special singers, some with their children, serenaded us with familiar carols. When they finished, I invited them inside for hot cider and cookies. Phil seemed to really enjoy seeing his friends. Although he wasn't able to really interact with them, it was obvious that he was pleased. I was so touched by their kindness, and it proved to be one of the most special times of the holiday season. I knew his friends sensed the gravity of the situation, but those concerns went unspoken, and we enjoyed visiting and celebrating the Christmas season.

After Phil's discharge from the hospital, he found it difficult to shower, shave, and get dressed by himself. He no longer had the strength to stand in the shower, so we incorporated the use of a plastic chair that enabled him to sit in the shower without the fear of falling. We had our routine down to a science. I would start the water, get the temperature regulated, and then help him onto the shower chair where he was able to balance the hand-held shower while he bathed. It usually took Phil 20-30 minutes to complete this routine. Once he finished, I would hand him a towel so he could dry off while still seated. When he was ready to get dressed, I would help him out of the tub and onto the closed toilet seat where he would sit to put on his clothes. At this point, he was also using a walker. Once he was dressed, I brought him his walker, and he would make his way to the den and onto the couch. For a while, every time he would get up and try to maneuver through the house, I was right beside him, so afraid he would fall.

Once I was more comfortable with his ability to ambulate, I stopped following him around. However, whenever I turned my head, he would try to go upstairs. With each attempt, I would explain to him again that it was for his safety that we were living downstairs. He would always say "OK," and then he would try again. I finally asked him if he realized he was confused. He looked at me and said "I'm not so confused that I don't know that you're taking really good care of me." It was so sweet because he had never acknowledged what I was doing for him. The location of his tumor didn't allow it.

December 23, 2011 9:25pm

When we were greeting people at our wedding reception 41 years ago (I know, Phil robbed the cradle), a woman came up to me and said, "The best advice I can give to you is to always keep your sense of humor." I have never forgotten that. Phil and I have laughed a lot over the years, and some would say at inappropriate times; however, even in the midst of great sadness, we have always been able to find humor in a situation. Phil is struggling right now from the cumulative effects of intense radiation and chemotherapy. He is having difficulty with short-term memory, and his legs continue to be extremely weak, a side effect of taking steroids. Exhaustion has taken its toll, and he sleeps a lot. But rest assured, Phil is still in the game. We continue to take it one day at a time as he attempts to regain his strength.

His next MRI is on January 30th. As our patience is tested, we know that God's timing is perfect. Our house will continue to be filled with laughter, especially as we prepare to spend the holidays with family and friends. On behalf of Phil, I wish all of you a very Merry Christmas.

Ecclesiastes 3:1-8

"For everything there is a season, and a time for every matter under heaven: a time to be born, and a time to die; a time to plant, and a time to pluck up what is planted; a time to kill, and a time to heal; a time to break down, and a time to build up; a time to weep, and a time to laugh; a time to mourn, and a time to dance; a time to throw away stones, and a time to gather stones together; a time to embrace, and a time to refrain from embracing; a time to seek, and a time to lose; a time to keep and a time to throw away; a time to tear and a time to sew; a time to keep silence, and a time to speak; a time to love, and a time to hate; a time for war and a time for peace."

Much love,
Shelly

Mary Chandler, Scott, and Louisa were at our house for Christmas. What fun it was to have them with us that morning as Louisa celebrated her first Christmas. Phil was doing better and seemed to enjoy all of the family activities that took place that day. Normally, we would leave Raleigh the day after Christmas to go to Montgomery to celebrate Christmas with Aynsley's family. Unfortunately, Phil's weakened condition would preclude our doing so this year. Fortunately though, Scott's parents have a lake house in Lake Norman, NC, and they offered to let all of us meet there to celebrate.

Aynsley and her family drove from Alabama, and the rest of us made the relatively short trip from Raleigh and Greensboro. Phil and I arrived at the lake house with all of the necessary equipment to ensure his comfort and safety. Although we had talked about making this trip, as we traveled down the highway, Phil turned to me and asked me where we were going. I felt so sad. He was in the car with me, yet he had no expectations; he had no clue what we were doing.

Our 4-day stay was so much fun! We had Christmas all over again, and Phil seemed to enjoy watching the 5 grandchildren open gifts. He sat in an oversized chair and just took it all in. Martha, our then 3-year-old granddaughter, had a very special relationship with Phil. She adored him and sat with him all the time. She loved to rub his bald head and at one point, as Phil sat asleep in the chair, Martha read to him from one of her books. It was so sweet but heartbreaking as I thought about the future. Phil spent a lot of time between the chair and the bed. If he wasn't asleep in one, he was asleep in the other. When Cade and the Alabama grandchildren said their good-byes to Phil, they had no idea it would be their last.

27

THE DOWNHILL SPIRAL

I have never been fond of roller coasters, especially emotional ones! After spending 9 hours at Duke today, we are back home, left to reflect on and process the information we received from Dr. V and his team. Phil spent the morning hours undergoing a series of cognitive tests as well as a driving test that was administered via the computer. We should hear the results of the driving test tomorrow with the results of the cognitive testing coming sometime next week.

The afternoon found us back in familiar territory, Clinic 1K, where Phil underwent the usual screening: checking vital signs, getting a weight, having blood drawn, and confirming his meds. After all of that, we met with the nurse practitioner who proceeded to tell us that the tumor was back. She showed us the MRI, and afterwards, Phil assured her that he wanted to keep fighting. She explained further treatment options; however, she told us it would ultimately be up to Dr. V to choose the most appropriate course of action for Phil. When she left to get Dr. V, we were trying hard to breathe what little air was left after it had been sucked out of the room by the news we had received. Phil was asking me questions I could not answer as we tried to reconstruct the conversation.

The next thing we knew, Dr. V was in the room telling us that he didn't think it was recurrent tumor after all but radiation necrosis. I reminded him that he had had the same thought last fall when the PET scan had proved otherwise. He said the only way we'll be able to know for sure is to wait until Phil completes a round of the new chemo regimen and has the next MRI. He said he would not order another PET scan because the treatment plan would remain the same.

Needless to say, my head felt like a pinball machine with thoughts, emotions, and questions bouncing back in forth in my mind. I can only imagine how and what Phil was thinking and feeling. With a new plan in our pockets (a chemo regimen I won't begin to try and explain except that it has something to do with platelets, growth factor and tumors), we set out for the treatment room where Phil received his bi-weekly dose of Avastin®. So it goes...we will continue to wait and to hope. I admire Phil's courage as he once again shoulders a blow and moves on.

As always, we thank you for your continued concern and for your prayers. We need them.

Love,
Shelly

Psalm 39:7 "And now, O Lord, what do I wait for? My hope is in you."

Phil wanted badly to go back to the beach, but I did not feel comfortable being there by myself with him. Dan and Courtney immediately came to our rescue and volunteered to go with us. Phil enjoyed it so much. Dan drove Phil on the beach and helped him navigate the stairs in our house. We ordered "take-out" and enjoyed beautiful weather for 2 weekends in a row. Dan and Phil smoked cigars, and we all pretended it was just another weekend at the beach. The peace of mind of having our best friends with us as Phil enjoyed what was to be his last days at our beach house was beyond description.

Throughout the month of January, I observed a gradual but obvious decline in Phil's condition. He was becoming more and more confused about small things. I tried hard to maintain his dignity so I didn't correct him when he would say things that didn't make sense.

One night after we had gone to bed, he continued to read his iPad. I asked him what he was reading, and he responded by saying he was checking out car insurance rates. What I didn't know until the next day when I received numerous phone calls from different insurance agents, was that Phil was requesting quotes for car insurance from each of their respective Web sites. I tried to find the humor in the results of his actions, but I did grow weary of explaining our way out of his requests!

One thing that remained constant throughout Phil's battle was his intense desire to continue working. His co-workers were unbelievable in their support of both Phil and our family. We worked out a plan where I would drop Phil off at his office for a couple of hours at least once a week where he would go through his mail and meet with his employees. Not only did this give Phil a sense of purpose, but it also gave me two hours to myself, which was a gift in and of itself. Phil felt empowered. He discussed business at the Credit Union and gave direction as though he were still in charge. His colleagues listened intently and assured him that they would execute his instructions. The relationship Phil had with his office staff and co-workers warmed my heart. The love he had for them was matched by the love they had for him. They were truly an extended family for all of us. Our wish was literally their command. Together, they played a large role in making Phil's final months special ones.

We received the results of Phil's driving test, and they were just as I expected - he failed miserably. I would be lying if I didn't say I was relieved to hear the outcome. He had been pressuring me to let him drive to the point where I actually hid the keys so that he would not sneak out and take a spin. His cognitive testing also showed significant decline in executive functioning. In the official report we received, the neuropsychologist recommended that the testing be repeated in 9 months. Although I knew that in 9 months there wouldn't be an issue, I used her recommendation to boost Phil's spirits. I proposed that we concentrate on his treatment protocol and that once it was completed it, we would again go for testing. He accepted my proposal.

28

UNCONDITIONAL SUPPORT

WE HAD A very close relationship with our brain tumor team and were encouraged to e-mail them with any questions we may have had. The freedom to communicate with them any time of the day was very comforting and I did so often. I could always count on a quick response. As Phil's condition became more precarious, e-mails to Christina became the norm. The following e-mail chain reveals the start of Phil's final decline.

Wednesday, February 1, 2012

Christina, it was so good to see you yesterday. As convinced as I was in December that Phil's MRI would show diffuse tumor and it did not, I was just as convinced yesterday that his MRI would be stable, and it was not. Although disappointing, we will continue our fight against Phil's GBM. After leaving 1K, Phil went upstairs and had his Avastin® treatment, and that went well. Because Debbie had already left for the day, we were not able to schedule Phil's next appointments for Avastin®, MRI, and 1K visits. Is that something I can request through you? Thanks Christina!

Hugs,
Shelly

Hey Shelly- I emailed Dr. Kirkpatrick also to get his opinion because Dr. V really thinks it could be from radiation. He hasn't emailed me back but I'll let you know what he says too. I have requested appointments on the following days: 2/14, 2/28, 3/31, and 3/27; all with labs and treatment room appointments. Do you look for Phil's appointments online or get the emails that they have been scheduled? Let me know by next Tuesday at the latest if you haven't been notified of any appointments. Are you doing ok? xoxox

Thank you so much Christina. I am OK. I simply don't have the energy to think past today. I still long for answers to questions that have no answers. If this is in fact tumor progression, is the timeframe we are working within the same as if Phil were not receiving treatment? I find myself sitting around thinking "is this going to be the day he will start falling again, is this the day he will become bowel incontinent, is the day he won't be able to walk?" I'm sure I am no different than anyone else. I just know that as long as Phil wants to fight this thing, I will be in the ring with him to love him and support him through the entire ordeal. I thought I had prepared myself for the results we heard yesterday, but it hit me hard. I try not to let my guard down around Phil because I am his cheerleader. My heart breaks for him, and there's not a thing I can do but be with him as he navigates his way through this nightmare. As you know, we love you and our team dearly, and are so grateful for the care and guidance you all provide to us.

Love,
Shelly

I think if this is true tumor progression it will continue to grow but much slower if the Gleevec® and Hydrea® work. If it doesn't work at all, then I would expect the tumor to grow much faster and we would see a decline in Phil within several weeks. We sent the prescription for the Gleevec® and Hydrea® to CuraScript. Sometimes there is a delay due to them wanting to cover it. If we don't know anything by next week we may go to plan B (Cytoxan®) and save the Gleevec® and Hydrea®. I will ask Elaine how soon is too soon follow up with CuraScript. We too will support Phil, and of course you, as long as he is in this fight, and even when he has decided he has had enough, we'll still be here.

Love,
Christina

Christina, first of all, we have not received any notifications regarding upcoming appointments. Second of all, I spoke with someone yesterday from the mail-order pharmacy who told me she is now sending the information to BCBS for approval of the chemo! We should hear something in the next 24-48 hours re: approval of the Hydrea® and Gleevec®. If they approve it, Phil will have been off chemo over 2 weeks. Should we expect a negative impact on Phil's condition because of the interruption of treatment? Also, have you heard anything from Dr. Kirkpatrick? Not that it makes any difference, but when you told us that there was tumor progression, were you just passing along the interpretation of the radiologist who read the MRI? Had Dr. V not looked at the MRI before then? I'm just trying to wrap my head around something that really doesn't matter. Either way, as Dr. V said, the treatment remains the same. Phil seems to be stable...maybe a little more incontinence, but no problems with ambulation. He remains confused about some things, but all in all he is doing OK. Thank you again Christina. I look forward to hearing from you.

Love,
Shelly

Hi Shelly,
Dr. K did not answer me back. Dr. V didn't think he would. I think we are ok until the end of the week waiting for the approval. If we have to begin an appeal process then we will most likely start the Cytoxan®. Also, I have followed up with the appointments, and you should hear something by tomorrow. You should get appointments for 2/14, 2/28, 3/13, and 3/27.

Monday, February 13, 2012
Hey Christina. When we got ready to go to bed, Phil could not get up off the couch. I had to call my brother and nephew over to get him up and onto the walker. They got him to the bathroom and to the bed. I'm worried about what we have in store for the night since he gets up 3-4 times to pee. See you tomorrow.

Friday, February 17, 2012
Christina, just checking in to say that Phil's ambulation is certainly better (no need for his walker), his head is not hurting, but he is 4+ crazy! He is so very, very confused. Do you think this is indicative of cerebral edema? Would you expect this to have improved after starting the Decadron®, or have I not given it enough time? Also, Tuesday night I gave him one of the Risperdal® and since he was asleep within an hour, I didn't give him another. Well, he got up 3X during the night. Last night I gave him 2 and he got up only once. I guess that's progress. If his mentation doesn't clear, would you think that means tumor progression? Is there criteria that would indicate the need for an MRI before his next scheduled

one? I hope that one day I will remember him when he wasn't sick. Thank you, Christina.

Love,
Shelly

Monday, February 20, 2013

Hey Christina. I hope your class was an interesting one and that you had a nice weekend. We had a CRAZY weekend, and I ended up calling Dr. V. As I had mentioned to you on Friday, Phil was getting progressively more confused. On Saturday, he was like a crazy man!! I mean he thought we were at our beach house, he said he was going to drive to Havelock to get biscuits (something we have NEVER ever done), he was wandering all through the house, picking up everything he saw and fiddling with it. He was talking absolutely crazy! Not one thing he said was making sense! That's when I decided I needed to call someone. Dr. V said the Gleevec® can affect the liver enzymes and perhaps that was what was going on with Phil. He told me to dc the Decadron® and to give him 4 Risperdal® right then (it was about 11:00). He said to give him 4 more at bedtime, which is what I did. I have continued that regimen, and although he is no longer 4+ crazy, he is still confused. My questions are as follows:

1. Should I continue with the 4 Risperdal® (0.5 mgs) bid? If so, I am going to need more soon. I guess I will need a new script so that insurance will pay??

2. Phil needs another script for the hydrocortisone.

3. Although Elaine told us that Phil should not have any problem with nausea, he doesn't want to take any chances, and he is taking Zofran® 8 mg bid, which I can't blame him for doing; however, we will need another script for Zofran® 8 mg. Insurance, for some reason, wouldn't cover the 4 mg last time I tried to fill it. Go figure.

As always, thank you. We're holding on by the hairs of our chinny chin chins.

Wednesday, February 22, 2012

Christina and Elaine, please help me, advise me, humor me... Phil has had 2 episodes of bowel incontinence since 4:00 this morning (he was on the floor when I woke up and I was able to get him upright and on the walker), and he just wet the bed through his depends. I am typing this as he continues to sit on the commode. He tells me his left leg is numb. Do I need to call hospice for an evaluation? I just need someone to tell me what to do. I don't know what this all means. Is this likely to become the norm now? I am really struggling.

Thanks so very much.

Monday, February 27, 2012

Christina and Elaine, we have just gotten home from Phil's MRI at Duke tonight, and I will be amazed if the results are "stable." Phil has had a significant decline today. It's as though he cannot process what I say to him. It's also like he has forgotten how to walk. It took me and a friend 20 min to get him into the car to go to Duke. When we arrived, it took 2 attendants about 10 min to get him out of the car. When we returned home, it took 3 people to get him out of the car and inside the house. My brother is spending the night with me because I am terrified that Phil will fall. Both of our girls will be here tomorrow. I will be anxious to hear what you all advise.

Thank you for all your help,
Shelly

29

THE END NEARS

February 28, 2012 8:39pm

Although I knew I would eventually have to make this post, I was hoping it would be a while before I would need to do so. It is with great sadness that I must tell you that Phil is losing his battle. Because he had begun experiencing an increase in symptoms characteristic of tumor progression, he had another MRI last night, some 4 weeks earlier than planned. When we saw the neuro-oncologist this afternoon, he informed us that Phil's tumor was ten times the size it was just a month ago. The tumor is so aggressive that it is simply not responding to any of the chemotherapeutic regimens. Therefore, the decision has been made to discontinue all treatment and to admit Phil to an in-house hospice facility in Raleigh. There will not be a bed available until tomorrow, so he has been admitted to Duke for the night. The plan is to transfer him tomorrow afternoon to Hospice of Wake County on Trinity Road. At this point, I think Phil is up for short visits, so those of you who would like, please stop by.

Phil is one of the bravest people I know. He has fought this battle with dignity, never questioning why he was stricken with such a merciless disease. My heart is broken, but I am strengthened by my faith, my family, my friends, and the countless prayers being said on our behalf. I will be forever grateful for the kind expressions of love and friendship.

Joshua 1:9 "I hereby command you: Be strong and courageous; do not be frightened or dismayed, for the Lord your God is with you wherever you go."

Love,
Shelly

Although December and January had their own challenges, the month of February was a living nightmare; Phil was getting sicker and sicker.

Throughout January and the first 2 weeks of February, Phil went to physical therapy twice a week. He was convinced it was helping him, so I supported him and encouraged him to keep challenging himself. I would sit in the waiting room and watch him work with the physical therapist. Instead of seeing progress in what Phil could do, all I saw was what he couldn't do. It was heartbreaking to see him working so hard in a futile attempt to strengthen himself.

During his clinic appointment on February 14th, Dr. V prescribed more steroids for Phil. I was prepared for the usual side effects, but this round made him crazier than ever!! Mary Chandler and Scott came to Raleigh to help me for the weekend, and Mary Chandler made the comment that if she had not witnessed her daddy's behavior, she would have never believed what I was telling her! Phil thought he was at the beach. He kept telling me he was going to drive to Havelock, NC and get biscuits. He also thought Dan was with him. He went outside and literally ran around the yard. Mary Chandler and I would watch from the kitchen window as Scott tried to keep up with Phil. He had never moved so fast, and we were so afraid he was going to fall. I immediately called

Dr. V and he changed the prescription and added another to calm Phil down. That afternoon he finally calmed down, and sat quietly for the rest of the day. We were exhausted from the activities earlier in the day, and the dialogue continued as we wondered what was going to happen next. Mary Chandler and Scott left on Sunday and once again I was left alone to deal with Phil. Just when I thought I couldn't be more worried and scared, I was.

From the time Phil came home from his hospital stay in December, we slept in the downstairs bedroom to minimize the risk of him falling on the stairs. There are 2 double beds in the room so Phil took one, and I took the other. By not actually being in the same bed with him, I felt that I "slept" a little bit better; however, each time he made a sound or got up to go to the bathroom, which was at least 4 times a night, I woke up. I would watch him make his way to the bathroom just knowing he was going to fall. I would offer to help him, but he would always say he was OK. I wanted to give him as much independence as I could, but doing so was more stressful for me. Sometimes he would use his walker and at other times he wouldn't. He'd always make it back to the bed where he would literally fall on the mattress. It seemed I would just be going back to sleep when he would get up again and the entire scenario would repeat itself. Phil seemed to do his best sleeping from 5:00 am-9:00 am, so I took advantage of that. I would get up at 7:00, have a leisurely breakfast, read the newspaper, check my e-mails, and then shower and dress. At 9:00, I would wake Phil. This would be his first call. By 9:30 he was usually up and ready to eat breakfast. Once he had a chance to eat and read the paper, we would tackle the shower, shaving and dressing routine. Each day he would tell me what to bring him to wear. It was always business attire, and I would have to explain to him that he wasn't going to work that day and that he could just wear jeans. He would always respond by saying OK. At that point, he would go into the den where he would remain for the rest of the day. His briefcase sat by the door always ready to go to work with him.

The one activity I continued to participate in was a Bible Study that met at our church every Monday night. This was a covenant group that had formed 4 years earlier, and I considered them my support group. My routine consisted of leaving the house at 6:40 to make the 7:00 start time. It was a 2-hr class, so I was usually home by 9:30 at the latest. I would always leave Phil on the couch with instructions to not do anything stupid. Phil would laugh and assure me that he would be fine. I would also tell Molly and Tapper that they were in charge, and that I expected them to keep Phil in line.

On Monday night, February 20th, I followed my normal routine. I always kept my cell phone close by in case Phil needed to get in touch with me. On this particular night, my phone rang at 8:20. Seeing that it was Phil, I excused myself and took the call. When I answered, no one was talking on the other end of the line. I could hear sounds of movement, but that was all. I kept calling Phil's name over and over again. My heart raced as I tried to get him to talk. He finally said "yeh." I asked him if he was OK and I heard "yeh." I said "Phil, have you fallen?" Again, I heard "yeh." I finally got out of him that he had fallen in his shop. I told him to remain where he was and that I would be right home. I told him I wanted him to stay on the phone with me as I traveled back home. He was determined to get up and make his way back to the house. He told me he was so cold and that he had to get back inside. I pleaded with him to stay where he was until I could get to him, but he refused. I was terrified that he would trip on the flagstone path back to the house.

As I drove home, I listened on the phone while he successfully navigated the many obstacles from his workshop back to the house. Once he told me he was back on the couch, I hung up the phone and tried to concentrate on driving. When I walked back in the house, I found Phil shaking from being cold. I felt so bad for him. He told me it had taken him 25 minutes after he fell to figure out how to dial my number. I knew then I wouldn't be able to leave Phil alone again. I simply could not trust what he might do or where he might go. There was no reason to scold him because he couldn't process what I was saying to him. In his mind, he hadn't done anything wrong. At that point, I was just relieved that he seemed fine physically. He had not hit his head, cut himself, or broken anything. I, on the other hand, was not OK. I was sick with worry. I wanted to know what I should do, if anything.

February 24, 2012 was Louisa's 1st birthday, and Mary Chandler and Scott were having a birthday party for her on Sunday afternoon, February 26th. I told Phil about it and gave him the option of going. He told me he thought he would just stay at home; I was relieved. It was difficult enough to care for Phil on our own turf, but taking him to Greensboro was more than I wanted to tackle. I made arrangements for my sister to come over and keep him company until my brother and nephew could get to our house later in the afternoon. The party started at 4:00. My plan was to leave Raleigh at 2:30, go to the party from 4:00-5:00, and be back home by 6:30. I was grateful to have 4 hours to myself even though two thirds of that time would be in the car.

I budgeted my time as I had planned, and I arrived home about 6:30. When I walked in the door, everyone, including Phil, greeted me with smiles. Seeing pizza boxes on the table, it was obvious what they had ordered for supper. I turned to Phil and asked him if he had enjoyed it. He responded "Yes, it was great!" I could see my brother out of the corner of my eye shaking his head from side to side. I walked into the kitchen where I saw Phil's plate. There were 2 pieces of pizza on the plate, and they hadn't been touched. When I asked Phil about it, he told me he thought he had eaten it. At that point, he got up, went to the kitchen, and poured himself a bowl of cereal. After eating his cereal, he also served himself a bowl of ice cream. Four hours later, he couldn't get off the couch.

When it was time to go to bed, I went through the usual routine of turning off the television, locking the doors, and letting the dogs out one last time. When I prompted Phil to get up, he couldn't do it. I tried my best to help him off the couch, but I couldn't get him to budge. When it became obvious that I wouldn't be able to move Phil, I once again called on my brother. He and my nephew Chris immediately came over and helped Phil get off the couch and to the bedroom.

Now I was witnessing Phil's decline in hours rather than days. We made it through the night, and the first thing I did the next morning was call our brain tumor team. I reported what had happened the night before, and I was advised to take Phil to Duke for an MRI that evening. It would be 4 weeks earlier than his next regularly scheduled MRI. Our appointment was at 6:00 and with the way Phil had been acting, I knew I would need to start moving him to the car earlier than I normally would. It was as though he had forgotten how to walk. He could ambulate with the help of his walker, but I had to be directly behind him, tapping the foot that needed to be placed in front of the other. He was just as happy as he could be. It didn't seem to bother him at all that he didn't know how to walk.

After we made it outside, I had to enlist the help of my neighbor, Robin to get Phil into the car. I wasn't sure we were going to be successful. After what seemed like an eternity, Phil was sitting in the front seat beside me, and we were on our way to Duke. I had notified Courtney that we were going to need some serious help in getting Phil out of the car when we got to the hospital. As soon as we arrived, Courtney was there to meet us. The two men she had enlisted to help must have pleaded with Phil for 10 minutes to swing his legs around so that they could help him out of the car. He sat there and just smiled, but he could not follow their instructions. I thought maybe it would help if he heard my voice so I joined in as well. Something finally clicked and Phil started moving his legs, making it possible for the men to get him out of the car and into a wheelchair. The same scenario, only in reverse, was played out after he completed his MRI. I don't remember how long it took to get him back in the car, but all I could think about as we drove home was how I was going to get him out of the car and into our house.

I called ahead to Robin, her husband Jon, and my brother and explained that I was going to need their help when I got home. I also asked my brother to spend the night with us, as I was really worried about what I might be facing overnight. When I pulled into our driveway, my helpers were waiting. It took all 4 of us to get Phil out of the car and into the house. Once inside, he was able to walk with his walker back to the bedroom. After an abbreviated version of his bedtime routine, Phil was down for the night. Dayle and I returned to the den where we talked until 1:00 am. I remember the time because the Daytona 500 was on and had been delayed by a fire on the track. Although I am not much of a NASCAR fan, we had gotten caught up in the drama that was taking place. We talked a lot about Phil and the situation at hand. I'll never forget Dayle saying to me "Shelly, Phil is a load. You can no longer care for him at home by yourself." I knew he was right, but I told him I wanted to wait and see what the doctors said when we returned for the results of his MRI. With that, we both went to bed.

I hardly slept. All I could think about was what I was going to do with Phil. My prayer had always been that the Lord would give me a sign so I would know when I could no longer care for him by myself. As much as I hated to admit it, I knew I had received my sign. For the first time in 18 months, Phil did not get up one time during the night.

The next morning Dayle came downstairs and told me he was going to go home, shower and change, run to his office for a few minutes, and then return to our house. Phil's appointment at Duke was at 12:30, and Dayle was planning on following us over and being present during our visit with the doctor. I called my sister and asked if she would come over and be at the house while I took my shower and got dressed. By this time, Phil was up and on the couch. I wasn't going to attempt to get him ready until after I had gotten myself ready for the day.

When Lyn arrived at our house, she walked in the den and saw Phil holding the newspaper upside down and acting like he was reading every word. She didn't say a thing about it.

Once I had finished getting ready, I made my way back downstairs. As soon as I walked in the den, I knew that Phil had had an accident. Bowel incontinence had become a problem for Phil during the past few weeks. I was able to get him to the bathroom where I cleaned him up and tried to think about what I could possibly dress him in. It's difficult at best, if not impossible, to dress an adult who cannot assist in any way. I finally decided on his golf rain suit. He already had on a t-shirt and his undergarment so I thought I would be able to slip the pants and jacket on without much of a problem. As I finished dressing him, Phil started sliding off the bed! I hadn't thought about the fabric being so slick. As hard as I tried, I could not keep him from going off the side of the bed. All I could do was scream for help and ease him down to the floor. We were in a mess. Phil was on the floor and the 5 people (Dayle, Lyn, Mary Chandler, Robin, and I) at our house could not get him up. Phil was not the least bit upset. Quite the contrary. He lay on the floor and just smiled. He could not assist us in any way as we attempted to get him up. Dayle volunteered to drive to the fire station 1/4 mile away and enlist the help of EMTs. I didn't want to call 911 and have firetrucks and ambulances with blaring sirens coming to our house. It wasn't 10 minutes before Dayle arrived back with 2 EMTs accompanying him. Those 2 people knew exactly what to do. They put their arms underneath Phil's and got him right up. With that, I asked them to go ahead and put Phil in the car. I couldn't take the chance of him falling again. I also didn't know how we would have gotten him in the car without their help. By the time all this happened, it was getting close to the time that we needed to leave. I fixed Phil his lunch and served it to him in the car. He had no complaints and just sat there and ate with no questions asked.

Once we got to the interstate and on our way to Duke, I called Christina, the nurse practitioner we would be seeing, and told her that I needed help. I explained that I could not bring Phil back home with me. He could not walk or follow simple instructions, and he was a major fall risk; I could no longer care for him by myself. At this point, she asked if I had left. I explained that we were on our way, and she asked if I wanted to know the results of the MRI. I told her I thought I knew the results and that was when she told me the tumor had grown 10 times its size since his last MRI on January 30th. I knew things were going downhill fast. I just wanted to get to Duke and have someone else in charge of the situation. I could not make another decision. I longed for someone to tell me what to do.

When we got to Duke, there were people to help Phil out of the car and into a wheelchair. I chose valet parking so that I could go on up to the clinic with him. They took us back immediately and placed us in a room. Dayle was there with me to write down everything that was said. It was comforting to have a second set of ears with me and even more comforting that it was my brother. Phil sat in the wheelchair with his head hung down and his eyes closed. Christina came in and greeted him. She pulled up his MRI on the computer just as she always did when reviewing it and showing it to us. She took one of Phil's hands as I held the other. She went on to explain the results to him and asked if he understood what she was saying. He responded by saying "I think you just gave me my death sentence."

Christina explained that none of the treatments were working, and there was nothing else they could try. She asked again if he understood. With that, Phil said "I think I do, but I wish I didn't." He was so flat that nothing seemed to phase him. I was crying hard as I held his hand, and he wasn't even aware. He asked to lie down so the medical staff helped get him on the exam table where he lay there with his eyes closed.

Dr. V came in, and all he could say to Phil was "Sometimes it's good to just be with God." I don't know what I was expecting, but I thought he would say more than that. I followed Dr. V out of the room where I found Christina and asked her point blank how long she thought Phil had to live. She answered "Shelly, it won't be more than 2 weeks." I was grateful for her honesty.

Shortly after Dr. V's visit, the social worker came by and explained that Phil could go to Hospice of Wake County, but there wouldn't be a bed available until the next day. The plan was for Phil to be admitted to Duke for the night and then be moved to Hospice the next afternoon. I felt like the weight of the world had been lifted off my shoulders.

Before Phil was moved to his room, the medical staff and allied health folks that had taken such good care of him over the past year and a half began coming in to say their good-byes. Two of Phil's favorites, Sarah and Lynn from the chemo lab, came by. The nurses in 1K, the nurse practitioners, and some of the other neuro-oncologists came by. It was very sweet, and although I am not sure if he was aware of what was going on, it meant a lot to me. Phil was finally moved to a room late that afternoon. We had made our first and last visit to the beautiful new Cancer Center at Duke.

For the 24 hours Phil was at Duke, most were spent sleeping. We made it through the night without incident. Because he was no longer able to change positions in the bed on his own, the nursing staff would move him every 3 hours. The next morning when breakfast was served, Phil said yes when I asked him if he wanted to eat. At this point, he was no longer speaking in sentences, but could answer yes/no questions. When I put a biscuit to his mouth, he didn't know to bite down. I tried coaching him through it, but he could not process my instruction. Even eating was becoming a difficult task to remember. As long as I broke food into pieces and placed them in his mouth, he was able to chew.

The morning was spent just passing time waiting for the ambulance service to come and take Phil to Hospice of Wake County. Dan came by to visit, but Phil slept through his stay. While Dan and I stood at his bedside, I broke down but quickly composed myself. I was emotionally and physically exhausted.

The ambulance service arrived at 1:00 pm right on time. They placed Phil on a stretcher and transported him to hospice just as planned. Both of us left Duke for the last time, Phil in an ambulance and I in my car.

Phil arrived at hospice about 30 minutes before I did, and Aynsley and Mary Chandler were there to greet him. Once I arrived, we met with the members of Phil's hospice team who walked me through policies and procedures. I signed the necessary paperwork and was handed a folder that included material that explained end-of-life care. The hospice social worker was wonderful and was willing to answer the myriad questions I had. There was information about funeral homes and cremation facilities, organ donation, and the actual stages of the dying process. Seeing the list of signs that the dying process was progressing somehow gave me a sense of control. It was all so surreal. For 18 months I had totally focused on trying to get Phil well; now I was focusing on helping Phil die. At this point, I was simply going through the motions. For the final time, all responsibility for Phil's care had been transferred to someone else. Unfortunately, what I was doing now was sitting, watching, and waiting for the signs that Phil was actively dying.

The meals menu for the day was posted on the bulletin board in Phil's room, but it took me a while to realize why one had to special order a meal. There aren't many patients still consuming food once they are admitted to hospice care. I asked Phil if he would like supper, and he responded yes. Ravioli was the featured item on the menu so I placed his order. When his meal arrived, he ate every bite I fed him. Once he finished, I went home to shower and change clothes; Mary Chandler stayed to keep Phil company. My son-in-law Scott was going to grab something for him and Mary Chandler to eat and then join them. The next thing I knew, Mary Chandler was calling me asking me what she should do. When Phil overheard her conversation with Scott about stopping at Char-Grill to pick up their supper, he placed his own order. Char-Grill was his favorite fast-food restaurant, and he had requested a Bar-B-Q sandwich and an order of fries! Mary Chandler asked what she should do, and I told her if Phil wanted it, to get it. Although he had just had ravioli, with Mary Chandler feeding him, he consumed every last bite of his second meal. With the exception of an Italian Ice a few days later, he never ate again.

As I mentioned earlier, when Phil was admitted to hospice, we were given an assortment of literature addressing end-of-life care and its associated issues. One of the pamphlets detailed the stages of dying and actual signs to watch for that would indicate the person was in the "active dying" stage. Each day, the girls and I would go over the list to see if we noticed anything. This was a new experience for all of us. I was filled with so many different emotions I didn't know how I felt. I was being faced with the imminent death of my husband, yet I was treating it as another checklist - which signs could I identify that Phil was actively dying; if he had a sign, what time frame were we to anticipate before it would lead to another sign? I was both comforted by having a list because of the pseudo-control it gave me over the situation, as well as terrified by the list. I had never been with anyone when they died, including beloved pets. Phil would always be the one to take the dog or cat to the vet if their condition warranted euthanasia; I would go to the mall so I didn't have to think about it. There would not be a mall to go to in this scenario. I would not be able to escape; I would be facing this death head on, but I wouldn't be alone. Aynsley, Mary Chandler, and Scott would be with me.

March 5, 2012 11:50 am

Phil is resting comfortably in beautiful surroundings at Hospice of Wake County. His room opens up onto a patio where it is landscaped with evergreens. At dusk, the deer make their way across the grounds. On Saturday, Phil was able to comment about how much he enjoyed looking outside. What a gift. As I write this message, our dog Molly is asleep on Phil's bed, providing unspoken comfort to her master. He has reached out and petted her, thereby making it known that he is aware of her presence. As Phil continues his journey, I would like to request that visits be limited to family and very close family friends. I want all of us to think of Phil and remember him as the robust, funny, and handsome man that he is and was. I am not sure how much longer we will have him here, but I am taking comfort in knowing that he is not suffering and that he is at peace. I know he can't be made whole on this earth, but he will be made whole in heaven. Saying thank you is just not adequate when I think of all the incredible love and support that has been provided to our entire family. I look forward to paying it forward. In the meantime, please honor Phil by continuing to perform random acts of kindness. You just never know what kind of battles people are facing and what a difference you can make in their lives.

With much love and appreciation,
Shelly

Phil loved his job and the people with whom he worked, and that sentiment was reciprocated by his employees and co-workers. His first full day at hospice was filled with visits from his Credit Union family. Although Phil had difficulty articulating conversation, it was obvious that he enjoyed seeing the countless people who came to visit. One of the highlights of the visits was the presentation of a handmade quilt depicting pictures of Phil and signatures of the people with whom he worked. The pictures and signatures had been scanned onto the fabric. In the middle of the quilt was a verse from the Bible, Philippians 4:13 "I can do all things through Christ, who strengthens me." What a precious gift. The woman who sewed the quilt together had worked furiously to complete it so it could be presented to Phil while he was still aware. Phil called it "my blanket," and he liked having it spread over him.

The visits continued for the next 5 days, but after Phil's level of consciousness started to diminish, we asked that visits be limited to family and very close friends. Throughout Phil's illness, preserving his dignity was always at the forefront. I didn't want people's last memory of him to be one of a disease-ravaged body, but rather one of a very handsome man with a quick smile. The reality of the situation was slapping us all in the face as we watched Phil slowly slip away.

I didn't want to leave Phil for a minute for fear that he would pass away while I was out of the room. The hospice staff had told us not to be surprised if that happened, as many times, people will wait until a loved one is out of the room before they died. I had worked out a routine where I would spend the night, have someone relieve me in the morning long enough for me to go home to shower and change clothes, after which I would return to Phil's room. After 4 days of this routine, the hospice staff approached me to discuss the possibility of my sleeping at home. They explained that not only did I need a break, but also Phil. They went on to explain that dying is a very intimate process and even though Phil was not conscious, his body could sense my presence. His body needed absolute silence and solitude as it continued the process of breaking down.

They assured me that I would be called if there was any perceived change in Phil's condition. It was difficult for me to comply, but I did. It had been months since I had slept in my own bed (we had been sleeping in the guest room downstairs since December), and I had to admit, it felt good.

March 9, 2012 4:51pm

The game is over, and Phil has won. He has now been made whole in heaven. He passed away peacefully at 4:20 this afternoon surrounded by his precious daughters, his son-in-law Scott, and me. There are just too many "thank yous" to be said. We will always hold close the many, many kind gestures bestowed upon our family. Our collective hearts go out to you in deep appreciation for loving Phil and for loving us through his 18-month journey.

2 Timothy 4:7 "I have fought the good fight, I have finished the race, I have kept the faith."

Love,
Shelly

I always loved Phil's hands. Because they were contracting, I was advised to remove his wedding ring so it would not have to be cut off later. Before doing so, I asked Aynsley to take pictures of his hands. Taking his wedding ring off was another reminder that our life together was nearing an end.

We continued to watch for all the signs we were told would signal progression of the dying process. At 11:00 on the evening of March 8th, Mary Chandler, Aynsley and Scott were preparing to leave hospice and return home for the night. As I was saying good-bye to them, Phil's breathing changed, and he began what is described as the "death rattle." It is a medical term that describes the sound produced by someone who is near death when saliva accumulates in the throat. With each breath, an ominous sound was produced. It was difficult to hear, but we were reassured that Phil was not in discomfort; it was just another sign of the dying process.

The hospice staff repositioned Phil and administered medication to reduce secretions in hopes of minimizing the "rattle." The next morning more signs were becoming apparent. His feet were cold, and his knees were a dark blueish red color. When I brought this to the attention of one of the nurses, she looked at me and said "You know Phil is now actively dying. If there is anyone that might want to see him again, you need to let them know." I made the appropriate phone calls to family, and I continued to watch and wait.

I was numb. I was on "death watch" but didn't really know what that meant. As I had so many times during Phil's 18-month illness, I wanted specifics, answers to questions that had no answers. Exactly how long would it be now? No one could tell us for sure, but we felt that Phil would be gone within 24 hours. Aynsley, Mary Chandler, Scott, and I sat in Phil's room surrounding him with as much love as possible. We let him know it was OK to go, that we would all be all right.

As the girls and I sat around Phil's bed, Aynsley noticed something different. I remember her saying "Mom." We all came closer, and it was obvious that Phil was breathing differently. I sent Aynsley out to get the nurse. When they returned to the room, it was obvious that Phil was taking his last breaths. The nurse listened with her stethoscope, and said "He's still here." In just 30 more seconds, her response was "He's gone." It was 4:20 in the afternoon, 9 days after Phil was admitted to hospice.

The nurse practitioner at Duke had been right - he had not lasted 10 days. Phil fought so hard to defeat a disease that just could not be defeated. What a blessing it was to be with Phil as he transitioned from his life on earth to his eternal life in heaven. All my fears of witnessing death had been quelled. I consider it a privilege to have shared this very private and intimate moment with Phil and our girls whom he treasured. We all kissed him good-bye one last time, gathered all of the things we had accumulated during Phil's stay, and headed home. Everyone's 18-month nightmare was over.

30

PHIL'S OBITUARY

PHILIP EDMUND GREER, 63, of Raleigh died on Friday, March 9, 2012. He was born in Morganton, N.C. to Ed and Aurelia Greer on December 30, 1948. Phil was a 1967 graduate of Needham Broughton High School and a 1971 graduate of UNC-Chapel Hill where he was a member of Sigma Nu Fraternity. He was an avid Carolina fan who took great pleasure in showing his Tarheel loyalty, especially while undergoing treatment at Duke University Medical Center. Phil enjoyed a 32-year career at the N.C. State Employees' Credit Union where he served as Sr. VP of Loan Administration. Preceded in death by his father, Ed Greer, he is survived by his wife of 41 years, Shelly Flammia Greer; daughters, Aynsley Greer Armstrong (Cade) of Montgomery, Al and Mary Chandler Greer Batchelor (Scott) of Greensboro, NC; grandchildren Mary Weldon, Greer, Martha, and Harris Armstrong and Louisa Batchelor; mother Aurelia Greer; sisters Pam Worth (Dave) and Frances Worsham (Mike). He is also survived by many nieces and nephews. A service celebrating Phil's life will be held at Hayes Barton United Methodist Church, 2209 Fairview Rd in Raleigh on

Monday, March 12, 2012 at noon. The family will receive friends at the church one hour before the service. In lieu of flowers and to honor Phil's memory, please consider a donation to Hospice of Wake Co, 200 Hospice Circle, Raleigh, NC 27607, Hayes Barton UMC, or The Preston Robert Tisch Brain Tumor Center, DUMC Box 3624, Durham, NC 27710. The family would like to express their heartfelt appreciation for the loving and compassionate care provided by the healthcare professionals in the Preston Robert Tisch Brain Tumor Center at Duke University Medical Center and Hospice of Wake County.

31

EPILOGUE

SHORTLY AFTER PHIL died, Courtney and I headed to the beach for a weekend with our bridge club. As Courtney drove, we began talking about the events of the past 18 months. She turned to me and said, "Shelly, did you really think Phil would survive?" I thought about my response, and then I began talking.

I explained to her that when it's your own loved one, your objectivity disappears. It didn't matter that I had the medical knowledge to know better; quite the contrary. It was my husband. In retrospect, it wasn't so much that I thought he would survive. What I did believe was that he would have his surgery, begin the protocol for treatment as outlined in the clinical trial he had been enrolled in, have his 33 radiation treatments and subsequent chemotherapy, and then life would get back to normal for a while. This was not to be.

Again, it wasn't because I didn't know otherwise, it was because my objectivity had flown out the window, and the only thing I could think about was getting Phil healthy again. All one hears when you cross the threshold of the Preston Robert Tisch Brain

Tumor Center is "At Duke there is hope." Unfortunately, my interpretation of that statement was mistaken. Throughout Phil's illness, I tried to understand what hope meant. At times, it made me angry to even see the word "hope." As we journeyed through our personal nightmare, hope became a 4-letter word to me. In fact, as the girls and I left hospice after everything was over, I instructed them to go home and throw away anything they saw around our house that had the word hope on it!

At that point, I was feeling anything but hopeful. I was feeling duped, taken advantage of, betrayed, lied to. You name it... any word other than one including the root word hope. It was a quote I read about 3 months after Phil passed away that finally put everything into the proper perspective and made sense to me. Per Gilbert K. Chesterton, "hope" is defined as the power of being cheerful in circumstances that we know to be desperate. This was a defining moment for me. I had been Phil's cheerleader for 18 months, always cheerful, trying to convince Phil that he was getting better, all the while knowing we were racing against the clock, and that his story would not have a happy ending. I was being cheerful in circumstances I knew to be desperate.

Phil has been gone for more than a year now, and the reality of my life is beginning to take hold. Phil was my anchor. I miss his presence. I miss the warmth of his body beside me in bed. I miss him telling me everything is going to be OK. I miss him giving me reassuring pats on my thigh, which was his way of saying "Don't worry about anything Shelly." I miss how he would give me a reassuring wink. I miss being hugged and held. I am no longer number one in anyone's life. There is no one at home to call and report all the funny things the grandchildren have done or talk to about other activities I am involved in. It doesn't make any difference how many people are around me; I am lonely. His loss has created a void that can't be filled.

I dream about him almost every night, but in my dreams, he is still a very sick man. I want so badly to remember him as the robust, handsome man that he was. I am told that with time, I will remember him as he was before he became ill.

For the 18 months that Phil was sick, I found myself saying that the fear of the unknown was consuming me; now I am saying the same thing but for very different reasons. I no longer have to worry about what the next day will mean for Phil in terms of how his disease will have affected him. Now I worry about what each new day will mean to me. Will I spend the rest of my life alone? Who will take care of me if I get sick with a catastrophic disease? I have children, but they have families of their own, and the greatest gift I can give to them is my independence. No one can comfort me like Phil did.

What am I going to do with myself? How do I redefine my life, myself, without Phil? I don't like saying that I am a widow. It's hard not being a couple anymore. I haven't been just Shelly since I was 16 years old.

I remember something someone told me during Phil's illness... try and imagine yourself in a car on a dark road. The headlights are on but only show so much of the road ahead of you. We're not meant to know everything that is in store for us; we must trust that there is a plan for our lives and that we will be shown our way as we need to see it. My adjustment and acceptance of my life without Phil can be measured in seconds and minutes and hours and days. The days are turning into weeks, and the weeks into months, and before I know it, the months will turn into years.

I know that time is my friend and that I am going to be OK. However, the void in my life is palpable, and I will always long for my life as it used to be when Phil was alive and healthy, and our family unit was whole. I will continue to rely on my faith. I will pray for direction and guidance, and I know that I will be all right.

Seven months after Phil's death, Mary Chandler and Scott were blessed with the birth of a second little girl, Katharine Chandler. There is nothing like the miracle of birth to give meaning to one's life. Katharine holds such promise, and she has given us all a new perspective. Life goes on in spite of personal struggles and heartache. I will honor Phil and everything he cherished by living my life anchored by my faith, my family, and my friends.

I have no regrets. I took good care of Phil and kept him at home as long as I could. As challenging and frustrating as it was for the 18 months Phil lived after his diagnosis, I would not change a thing about our approach to his disease. We simply did the best we could do in the midst of the worst of situations.

I loved Phil deeply, and I take great comfort in knowing that I too, was loved until the end.

Shelly and Phil in happier times (2009)

Shelly and Phil, with friends Courtney and Dan, celebrating Phil and Dan's 60th birthday on Alaskan cruise, 2009

Louisa Greer Batchelor's baptism, October 2011

Shelly and her family, Summer 2014, daughters Mary Chandler and Aynsley, and grandchildren Mary Weldon, Louisa, Katharine, Harris, Martha, Greer

Philip Mac Batchelor (Mac) and William Edmund Batchelor (Web)
born October 31, 2014.

BIO

SHELLY FLAMMIA GREER lives in Raleigh, North Carolina, and is the mother of two daughters and the grandmother of eight. She earned a BS degree in Health Education from the University of North Carolina at Chapel Hill and worked in a variety of health-related positions for many years. In 2010, she accepted an early retirement package from her employer of over nineteen years, GlaxoSmithKline, just months before her husband Phil, was diagnosed with a malignant brain tumor.

Crossing the Caring Bridge: A Journey of Hope and Despair is Greer's first book, a memoir she wrote as a means of catharsis after her husband lost his eighteen-month battle with a glioblastoma multiforme.

Made in the USA
Lexington, KY
02 March 2015